ROADMAP TO EASE

ROADMAP TO EASE

Release What Weighs Your Down
Embrace What Lights You Up

e'Layne Kelley

Muddy and Perfect Press
St. Petersburg, Florida

Roadmap to Ease

The author provides general practices and suggestions to enhance the reader's life and nurture their body, mind, and spirit. It's crucial to understand that this information is not a substitute for mental health counseling or the guidance of healthcare professionals. The author strongly encourages the reader to reach out for the support they feel most comfortable with, as it can facilitate profound healing and a sense of well-being.

Cover design and art by e'Layne Kelley
The Heartstrings Raven is by artist Beth Kauffman
All other art by e'Layne Kelley

To my son, Ian Koenigsberg...
my greatest blessing and dearest friend.

I love you to the moon and back...
and into infinity.

Your Roadmap

Acknowledgments

A huge thank you to my three editors. Valerie Clark, thank you for being so encouraging and for teaching me always to end a chapter with a couple of sentences to introduce the next chapter. Wonshe, thank you for being masterful at rearranging content so it found its rightful place in my book. Your idea to switch Chapters 1 and 2 was brilliant! Francesca Donlan, what fun to meet my final editor, who became an instant friend. Your enthusiasm for the content in my book and how it spoke to you was icing on the cake. You gave me the energy to make it to the finish line!

I am deeply grateful to those who listened to my ideas and provided unwavering support as this book evolved. Ian Koenigsberg, Kathy Mick, Michael Leaman, Catherine Woods, Angie Gregory, Cheryl Miller, Dave Schaefer, Terri Patrin, Lora Lee Davids, Lily Boynton Kaye, Patricia Wooster, my beta readers, and all my other cheerleaders, your encouragement was a constant source of inspiration. Thank you to all the women in Gain the Wisdom Sisterhood Tribe on Facebook. You walked this path with me for many years.

Thank you to The Anaïs Nin Trust and Ohio University Press for granting permission to use Anaïs Nin's quote.

The NOAA Office of Coast Survey, www.nauticalcharts.noaa.gov, provided the nautical map on my front cover; thank you! It shows the area where I grew up and where many of the stories in my book took place.

Loving Thanks to these creative and generous people:

The amazing people at Happy Self Publishing who lovingly typeset my manuscript. Analie and Sushmitha were jewels to work with.

Artist Beth Kauffman for the use of The Heartstrings Raven.

Amanda Boekhout is the model who inspires my art and graces this cover.

Talented musician Trapper Schoepp, thank you for sharing a great story that became my introduction.

Jenn of Joyful Hearts Designs, for permission to use the beautiful paper on the back cover.

MEDITATE
Live Purely
BE QUIET
Do your work with mastery
LIKE THE MOON,
COMe OUT
from behind the clouds!
SHINe
— Buddha

A Vast Familiar Place

If I choose to quiet my mind
I watch thoughts as they fly by
...on wings of birds, out open windows

thoughts with no container
mind with no judgment
dropping me into a vast, familiar place.

e'Layne Kelley

This Isn't Fun Anymore

I made it through concert security and walked into the lobby, where I saw the merch table for the unknown-to-me opening act, Trapper Schoepp. There were only two shirts for sale on the wall, and one read, "This isn't fun anymore." What could that mean? I thought. Maybe he is tired of being away from his family, schlepping stuff from town to town, and tired of living on a tour bus.

Not giving it another thought, I went to my front-row seat. Trapper was delightfully adorable, a gifted songwriter, and the youngest musician to share co-writing credit with Bob Dylan. At the end of his concert, he invited the audience to meet him at his merch table and then shared the story of the seeming out-of-place tee. Trapper said he was recently at a carnival riding a giant Ferris wheel. A distressed young man in the bucket seat below him kept saying, "This isn't fun anymore."

How often do we say this isn't fun anymore on the Ferris wheel of life? What do we do that makes us feel that way? Maybe we had one too many drinks the night before and lost the next day to a hangover. Possibly, we started a diet and promised ourselves we'd eat well, only to disappoint our hopeful spirit and give up a week later. Perhaps anxiety and stress are constant companions, and we are tired of feeling unfocused and restless. Or maybe we're having existential angst because we sense there is more to life than we realize, or we hear what calls to us, but we're in inertia's grasp. No, this isn't fun anymore.

We often believe that simply exerting willpower to change our outer lives will help us achieve weight loss, more focus, or less restlessness, ultimately leading to true happiness. However, when we rely solely on exerting our willpower to change behaviors, we can create a cycle of unresolved inner conflict. True happiness is found when we peel back the layers of our socialized selves and awaken to the rich, spiritual essence of our infinite being.

Our life can be likened to a Ferris wheel, especially when we consider how we function from our subconscious mind 95% of the time. Just as the Ferris wheel follows a fixed, predictable course, most of our behaviors respond on autopilot, running on an operating system to which we have no immediate access. These beliefs and behaviors were formed long ago and shaped by our socialization and past experiences. They keep us within our comfort zone and stop us from exploring dreams and new possibilities. Luckily, you'll learn to recognize the trappings of the subconscious mind and rewire your brain to support you in creating your best life.

Just as in daily life, we experience a range of emotions when riding the Ferris wheel. Excitement and anticipation stir in us as we ascend, and anxiety might visit us on the descent. Life has its highs and lows. The teachings in this book help us not get stuck on an emotional rollercoaster but find calmness as we breathe into feelings and let them move through us.

The view on a Ferris wheel always changes. The view is limited at the bottom of the rotation, and the landscape is dense. We watch people eat cotton candy, parents push their kids in strollers, and teens run to the next amusement ride. As we view this hustle and bustle of life, we're generally lost in thought, our minds narrating what we see. At the top of the Ferris wheel, we see the world view from a broader perspective. The clouds are billowy and endless; we feel the air blowing through our hair and the sun's warmth on our faces. To experience life in the present moment, you'll be introduced to the Watchful Observer, your constant companion. You will learn to view life from infinite awareness and perceive the spaciousness in which every experience unfolds.

On life's Ferris wheel, the rider doesn't have control over the machine's workings, which are determined by the operator and the machinery. Because of the randomness of this existence, we can feel like passive participants on life's journey. Just as we don't know what mechanisms make the Ferris wheel work, we don't know the workings of our body and how its automatic operating system can adversely affect our behavior. When we gain knowledge of how we respond to situations because of our primitive wiring and chemical responses, we become less reactive to involuntary impulses. As a rider on this magical, mystical tour called our life, I know there is much we have no control over, and most of what we worry about never happens. Life becomes more enjoyable when we learn to accept 'what is.' Practices are taught that will help you break through inertia to change what you can.

It's time to get off the Ferris wheel and move beyond the self-imposed limitations constraining you. You will learn to recognize them as you become the Watchful Observer of your reactions to daily life situations. Exploration beyond your comfort zone will foster growth and greater awareness. Simple mindful practices and probing questions will spark curiosity about why you do what you do and help you take life less seriously. Life in the present moment eliminates searching for something outside yourself. Your inner life becomes rich, and your outer life will be more joyous as you unencumber yourself from things that cloud your highest good.

Why This Book?

In my early twenties, I was incapable of feeling genuinely relaxed in my body, unable to find true peace of mind, and didn't know my life's purpose. However, I did have a few clues as to the cause of my restless discontent. I knew my thoughts had something to do with not feeling good enough...along with several other not-enough, like pretty, thin, lovable, and smart. I also experienced a quiet, reverent place within that used to be easily accessible as a child but was MIA. Like any good detective, I was hell-bent on following the clues to find a deeper meaning to life and, more importantly, a reprieve from my punishing and overactive mind. When I finally began to thaw from emotional numbness, fear, resistance to change, rigid beliefs, and creative blocks, I was just barely brave enough to dismantle my life as I knew it and put faith in something greater than myself. I surrendered to the creative flow of life, the universal oneness, and never looked back.

In this teaching memoir, I disclose parts of my journey to share what I've learned over decades by peeling back the layers of made-up stories and bogus beliefs. I found that if I shifted my focus away from self-obsession and meditated to calm my mind and feed my soul, I was met with peace along life's route. The path of awakening is a journey, not a destination. We may learn something profound only to forget it a week later, and that's OK. Life is a process of letting go of what we are not; what remains is who we truly are.

This book contains teachings I practice and aha moments I've experienced over six decades. No matter what my life's work was, training crisis counselors to work with disaster victims, managing an art park, or teaching art retreats, I shared what I'd learned about how to have a creative life of ease and how to let go of the burdens we carry.

I wrote *Roadmap to Ease* because I found freedom from my thoughts and misinformed beliefs and wanted others to do the same. This book is filled with information and practices I wish I had in my early twenties and stories of how I negotiate life when it gets difficult. It's important to know we are not the only ones feeling scrambled and alone. Sharing our authentic and transparent selves and our journey to peace and happiness shines a light on those experiencing darkness.

Where to Begin?

Awakening to the fact that we are not our thoughts and gaining distance from them is a brilliant place to begin. This Zen story offers a way to keep thoughts at bay. One day, a troubled young man named Bodhi was overcome by negative thoughts, a cluttered mind, uncertainty, and anxiety. He went to see a Zen master and asked him how to calm his troubled mind. The Zen master and Bodhi walked to a nearby river and sat on the bank. The master gave Bodhi a handful of leaves and told him they represented his thoughts. He instructed Bodhi to throw a leaf in the river every time he had a thought, whether the thought was pleasant or troubling. Bodhi threw leaves into the river one by one and watched them float down the river.

Bodhi sat quietly as the Zen master quietly spoke, "Learn to detach from your thoughts and do not judge them as good or bad. You are not your thoughts, and if you don't give them attention, they will float by like leaves on the river of life."

Bodhi realized he was breathing more rhythmically, and his mind was quiet. He experienced nature enveloping him as he sat peacefully with the Zen master, basking in the present moment.

Baby Steps Create Quantum Change

If you are familiar with my teachings, you know I am a huge fan of baby steps. Dreams drown in the tidal wave of grand expectations. Do you overwhelm yourself with unrealistic goals and throw in the towel when they are unmet? Disappointment, anxiety, and discontent result from over-expectation. Life happens in the present, not when we achieve a goal. Savor life's journey on the road to ease and awakening. Instead of getting lost focused on the end game, experience the momentum of baby steps, utilizing them to move toward your true north, your soulful self.

Have you ever seen a house jack? They are small, many the size of an empty paper towel roll. How does a house jack relate to baby steps? You can crank the mighty house jack a tiny bit, creating enough momentum to lift tons, resulting in quantum change. Don't let apathy or repetitive behaviors seize most of your waking hours. Set a timer for a few minutes and do a simple task or practice. Engaging momentum is a game changer.

My Promise

Our mortal life is short, and every person's journey is hugely significant since we all have something to share with the world. We only have so many heartbeats, and the ball is in our court regarding how we spend them. In this seemingly random, infinite universe, we do get to choose how we spend our life energy. If you want to choose more ease, less anxiety, and a deeper sense of your soulful self, you are in the right place.

What am I hoping to contribute to by writing this book? I share wisdom, tools, life experience, and the roadmap to move beyond self-limiting thoughts and beliefs by illuminating your soul's path. This book is overflowing with practices leading to a happier, more peaceful, awakened life. I can promise your life will be richer, and you'll experience more freedom as you co-create with the universal flow, but there is a big "if."

To fulfill my promise, I need you to get excited (or at least interested) about practicing the tools and shifts contained in these pages. You cannot expect profound life changes if you use this information simply as an intellectual exercise. You might read about healthy and unhealthy ego characteristics. Still, until you investigate your past and watch your current behaviors to reveal your patterns, the ego traits are just words on paper. It is helpful to know why we do what we do, but practice is necessary for change to occur, like rewiring our brains. To leave our comfort zone of rote behaviors and unexamined beliefs and embark on the awakening adventure, it's imperative to form new habits through repetition.

Practice is the key to alleviating suffering's pitfalls so you can fully embrace life in the present moment. The good news: it's not a race. There is no finish line or right or wrong way to practice. You will learn to observe your thoughts, beliefs, behaviors, and life experiences and decide if your actions weigh you down or light you up. You will ask yourself, is this coming from a place of fear or love, and am I moving toward ego or divinity? You observe the direction you are moving and what that feels like, then choose whether to shift your behavior.

If you only do one practice in this book for the rest of your life, like bringing your attention to your breath, your life will improve. You will become less reactive and live more in the present instead of the past or future. Remember, curiosity and humor are your friends on this journey. Curiosity will make you more engaged in life, and levity will brighten your day.

We don't know what life will bring, but it's usually a combination of happy and challenging times. Unsaddling yourself from the restraints of your upbringing and putting to bed well-worn stories that don't serve you will reward you with ease and happiness. And when illness, tragedy, and loss break your hearts wide open, these challenging times will be a little less bumpy if you take the time to embody these teachings. You will have the tools to navigate the inevitable pain life can bring, even in the most turbulent times.

I must be a mermaid, I have no fear of depth and a great fear of shallow living."
- Anais Nin

what do
you
want to
pack
for your
life's
journey...
what do
you
want to
leave behind?

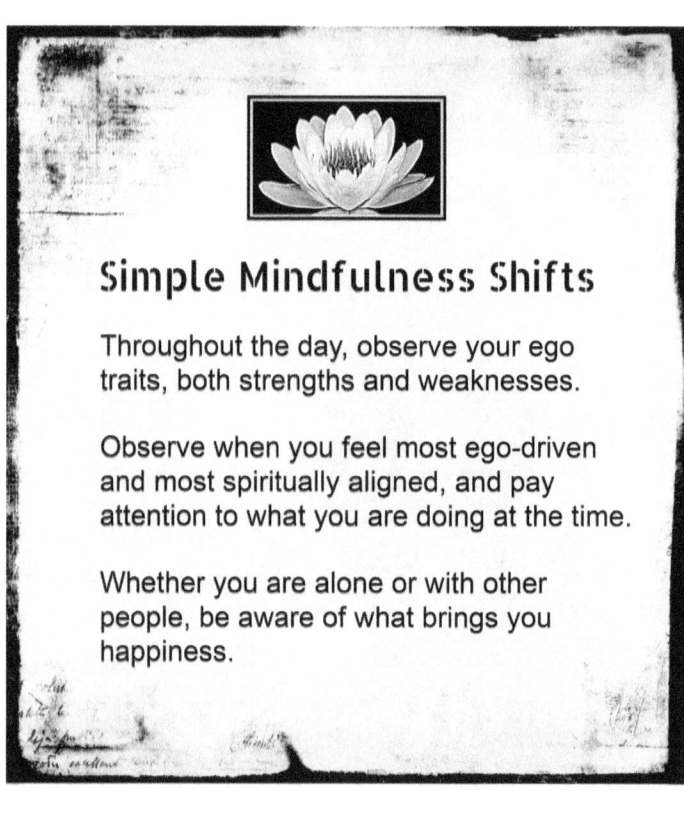

Simple Mindfulness Shifts

Throughout the day, observe your ego traits, both strengths and weaknesses.

Observe when you feel most ego-driven and most spiritually aligned, and pay attention to what you are doing at the time.

Whether you are alone or with other people, be aware of what brings you happiness.

Waking Up to Your Divinity

"There is a candle in your heart, ready to be kindled. There is a void in your soul, ready to be filled. You feel it, don't you?"

– Rumi

Converging Miracles

I always believed I would die young. My father died at 25 – one month after I was born, and I never thought I would outlive him. This belief may have fueled my thirst for drugs and alcohol because something drove me hard and fast toward an early death.

Around midnight, in the fall of 1975, I left a neighborhood bar in St. Petersburg after stopping to play a couple of games of pool and climbed into my green MG Midget. I hit third gear and headed down a familiar road. Suddenly, the double lines in the center of the road disappeared, and my car flew off a cliff and into the air.

"I am going to die," was the last thought that I had before I flew off a 50-foot cliff and lost consciousness.

When I woke up in the hospital, I knew it was a miracle I had survived. I learned that an enormous crater was dug to construct the infrastructure where the interstate was being built. The road I traveled had an open-to-local traffic sign and was not blocked off where it ended.

Two EMTs had parked their ambulance in the lot overlooking the construction site to smoke a joint. Imagine their surprise when their pot break turned into a rescue mission!

Because it was a Friday night, it's unlikely I would have been found before Monday morning when the construction crew arrived.

The surprise rescue wasn't the only blessing. A week before the accident, I had returned from Jamaica, where a 151-proof rum-induced hangover ended my desire for cigarettes. The gas tank leaked when I crashed, so if I had been smoking, the car would have gone up in flames. To add to this, the week before the accident, I traded cars with my friend – my Volkswagen for her Midget. The Midget's front engine buffered the impact, unlike the rear-engine Volkswagen would have done. This convergence of miracles left me feeling blessed to be alive.

This near-death experience sparked a profound spiritual awakening. There had been another "me" at the scene – a calm presence observing "me" driving off the cliff. That presence had no fear or judgment about who was driving off the cliff. That me, who was witnessing the one driving off the cliff, wasn't dying. That me had the same quality I had experienced in my youth; a spacious awareness, peacefully untethered from my everyday reality and thinking mind.

After I woke up, I wanted to find that kind of peace again. Being hurled off an interstate highway under construction and plummeting 50 feet seemed like a compelling reason to make some changes. Escaping death pushed me to confront my hollow lifestyle and evaluate my life's purpose.

While I experienced a profound shift in consciousness, my resurrection from an unhealthy and unfulfilling lifestyle didn't happen overnight. I began by taking responsibility for my choices. First, I realized the story about dying young wasn't serving me, and I released that belief. Instead of letting life unfold without direction, I became an active participant, steering my life's course.

Adopting a healthy diet became my primary goal. During a five-week cross-country trip from Florida to California, I read *A Good Cook – Ten Talents*, a health manual filled with vegan recipes.

Despite eating healthier, I had emerging health issues. When I left to drive back to Florida, I felt increasingly ill. My travel buddies noticed the whites of my eyes were bright yellow, so we stopped at a hospital in Texas. The doctor told me that I most likely had hepatitis, but there was nothing he could do for me.

Once I got back to Florida, I immediately went to another doctor, who confirmed that I did have hepatitis. Since the medical world offered no treatment at that time, I researched a protocol for regaining my health. I learned lecithin aids liver repair, so I treated myself with that. I also ate whole foods. Within a short time, the jaundice disappeared, my strength returned, and the doctor gave me a clean bill of health.

For 20 years, my hepatitis diagnosis remained a distant thought. (Until I was 40 years old, I had no clue this life-threatening disease was replicating in my body.) In fact, my quest to become radiantly healthy became a priority. I began running, but despite no longer smoking, running burned my lungs. So, I started jogging slowly and marked my daily progress by the number of mailboxes I passed. The first few days, I could only make it past a few, but I happily made it around the block within a week. The journey toward health required discipline and baby steps. Even though I had a long way to go, I began paving the road to a happier, healthier life.

As I started to feel more alive, I realized that somewhere between puberty and adulthood, I lost my innocence and intrinsic creative flow. Some of my earliest and fondest memories were as a 6-year-old designing clothes with my Nana. Later, my mother and I took numerous ceramic and sewing classes and created intricate mosaics with tiles we collected. During high school, art became my passion. Afterward, I attended junior college and majored in art.

In my first art class, the teacher gave us an assignment to draw an egg. I raised my hand and told him I wasn't inspired to draw an egg. He didn't care and told me I was in the wrong class. I walked out. I don't know if I had an undeveloped sense of curiosity, lacked the discipline required to do the assignment, or if I just needed more freedom of creative expression. Whatever the reason, my re-emerging creative spirit was once again squelched. I changed my major to sociology.

My college years helped develop my mental discipline but never extinguished my desire to create art. In fact, it beckoned relentlessly. For two years, I stared at a blank canvas and a pile of colorful paint tubes – unable to open them or paint a single brush stroke. The burdens I dutifully carried along life's journey – perfectionism, procrastination, indecision, and fear of being judged immobilized my artistic voice and creative passion. Still, a stirring inside me wouldn't let the weight of these burdens settle into my bones. A distant whisper assured me that freedom from my mind's incessant chatter was possible. But at that time, I didn't know how to free myself.

Even though a deeply buried "knowing" compelled me to seek spiritual knowledge, the veils between the worlds of my inner life and outer life hung heavy. I had no idea what mysteries would be revealed when they lifted. But most often, runaway thoughts drowned out the distant whispers. So many thoughts fought for dominance in my mind that it felt like a massive group of Black Friday shoppers trying to squeeze through the small doors at Wal-Mart first thing in the morning. Monotonous scripts demanded my attention, distilled to two repetitious refrains: "Why am I unable to live a creative, happy, peaceful life? Will I ever get past obsessive negative and self-loathing thoughts?"

Little did I know then that this constant negative noise was just the tip of the iceberg. Later, I began to understand that the psychological issues driving me were buried deep below the surface.

One of those issues concerned my relationship with food. My blocked creative energy manifested in my obsession with food. My mind engaged in an endless loop of negotiations. The relentless mental chatter and body-loathing while bargaining with food wore me down.

"Will I make muffins? If I make muffins, how many will I eat? Should I fast? How can I lose the fat on my thighs?"

Though I tried to change these thoughts and behaviors, my willpower was no match for food's power over me. Eventually, I was in enough mental torment to seek peace from my punitive mind. I began to study with Sufi master, Pir Vilayat Inayat Khan, a gentle and wise man. His practices felt like a radical departure from the Catholic Church and my Catholic school upbringing.

After earning my BA in sociology, I made several sojourns to The Abode, the spiritual sanctuary and retreat center in Hudson Valley, New York, that Pir Vilayat Inayat Khan founded. While there, my diet became a meditation, as did working in the garden and spending hours in silent retreats. A new Nikon camera was my constant companion, inviting me to slow down and pay attention to the details of the world around me. Meditation practices helped me develop an observant mind, and my thoughts quieted. During one of my last stays at The Abode, I "heard" a message instructing me to leave my comfortable life in Florida and venture into the unknown.

I chose to listen.

After I left New York and returned to Florida, I put my belongings in storage, quit my job, found a home for my beloved cat, and left my adorable beach cottage that had been my long-time home. With no money in the bank, no job waiting for me, and no Plan A, much less a Plan B, I hit the road with a sweet friend in his Volkswagen camper with fear and excitement in my belly.

I left knowing the only way to break through the immobilizing fear that controlled my thoughts was to confront them head-on. I chose to push aside fear and take the leap. I put my trust in something unknown and greater than the familiarity of my discontent and self-loathing thoughts. After zigzagging across America with my friend, we parted ways in Walnut Creek, California.

Alone and jobless, my new life began with little more than the clothes on my back and $500 available on a credit card. The blank canvas I had been unable to paint for years was mirrored in the blank canvas of a life before me. This time, inaction was not an option. I chose to craft a creative and spiritually aligned life that would lead me toward happiness.

Dark Night of the Soul

In hindsight, I realized that the decision to leave St. Petersburg and the time leading up to that decision was my dark night of the soul. The life I had constructed there provided ease and beauty, and although I had embarked on a spiritual journey, there was still a heaviness, weariness, and despair weighing me down.

I knew in my bones that a leap of faith was required, and I argued with that knowing most of the time. The voice I heard at The Abode confirmed that I needed to take flight from my comfortable nest and leave my past behind. I pared down all my belongings, packed a small bag, and sprang into the unknown with faith and terror stirring inside. Behind me was the death of all that I thought I knew. Before me was blind faith, a heart filled with devotion, and a commitment to dutifully follow the path I would be shown.

"Dark night of the soul" has long been used to describe the experience of going through a painful and profound spiritual awakening. Usually, it is a time when one feels alone, disconnected, empty, or hopeless, and life seems to be without meaning or direction. Sometimes, a dark night experience is brought on by a significant life trauma or a diagnosis of a life-threatening disease. During this painful period, the framework around one's life splinters and becomes unhinged. The very construct – the meaning given to one's life – no longer makes sense.

A dark night is temporary and can last a few months or a few years. It's a natural season of life, a time to release what no longer serves us, a time to awaken our inner life, and a time to move in a different direction.

Carl Jung said, "There is no coming to consciousness without pain. People will do anything, no matter how absurd, to avoid facing their own soul. One does not become enlightened by imagining figures of light, but by making the darkness conscious."

As one experiences a dark night, one's ego clings tight. But going through the darkness is the only way to come out the other side. It can be terrifying to navigate this unfamiliar terrain. Lessons await, and onerous questions echo in the darkness, begging to be answered. Who am I? Why do I suffer? Why does humanity suffer? What is the meaning of life? Is there a God? Do I have a purpose? Does any of this have a purpose?

Do these questions reverberate in your mind? Can you sit quietly with no distractions and feel peace? Have anxiety, restlessness, depression, and dissatisfaction become frequent companions? Is something missing from your life that material possessions, money, or losing that extra weight won't satisfy? Are you waiting for the right partner to make you feel complete?

Does your day unfold with ease in alignment with a sense of purpose, or do you feel like there is something more to life just outside your grasp? Is your outer life in control? Do you take time to nurture your inner life by meditating, getting curious, and practicing self-care? If the dark night of the soul resonates, or you have days that are bumpy and lonely, you're in the right place to recognize and dim the ego's deception so divinity can shine. This book is for you.

Soul Hole Repair

From third to eighth grade, I attended a Catholic school where Mass was required six days a week. That's logging in a lot of church time! Mass was conducted in Latin, which I didn't speak, so my young, creative mind needed distractions. Before Mass, I would donate money to light candles and throughout the service, I remained captivated by their dancing flames and refracting light from the stained-glass stations of the cross.

Morning Mass became my time to daydream and make up my own religious beliefs. My vision of sin was that it appeared as a soul hole in my solar plexus region. I "saw" grace as a fluffy green moss covering the entire area surrounding the soul holes. Since I was a good kid, I would make up sins to confess. I still haven't figured out what my innocent, young self was trying to repair. But in my mind, I filled my holes with "grace." My quest to repair soul holes felt existential, like I was trying to save the damned, those languishing souls I learned about in Catechism from the eternal flames of hell. I grappled with the concept that a loving God would send souls to purgatory or hell. This contradiction arrested my ability to believe what I was being taught.

The concept of soul holes that my young daydreaming mind created never left me. I believe we aren't born with soul holes, but they form from big and small traumas experienced during our lifetime. To this day, I feel deeply passionate about the concept of soul holes and their repair. These holes sever our connection to the divine, causing the development of both healthy and unhealthy ego characteristics to cope with being untethered from our souls.

We can acquire soul holes at a very young age and start to build armor around our fragile hearts. I recall a time in St. Augustine, Florida, while eating lunch in a cafe with my then-husband and our young son while on vacation. A "man of the cloth" sat at the table beside us with his wife and child. After his son did something he didn't like, he stood up, towering over the child, yelled at him, and bopped him on the head. I will never forget the look on that child's face. His embarrassment, shame, and fear were palpable. The cannon located across the street in the long-defunct fort may as well have blown a hole right through that tender little boy's soul. This kind of internalized pain and trauma is recorded in our subconscious mind and in our bodies. We either do the work to recognize and repair it or continue to suffer, sometimes adopting harmful beliefs and behaviors to fill the soul hole. Giving yourself grace and compassion is essential as you recognize and release the wounds and shame from your past.

Get Familiar with the Ego

The ego helps us navigate who we are; it's our self-image and the knowledge that we are separate from other people. Our ego identity is the compilation of stories we tell ourselves about ourselves and the beliefs we think our caregivers have about us. We identify with our bodies and things like our names, possessions, accomplishments, religion, physical appearance, and beliefs. The ego allows us to function daily in our communication, decision-making, and understanding of the world. The ego is neither negative nor positive and only becomes a thorn in our side when we are attached to our identity and believe we are our ego. Our self-worth is tethered to things that are transitory instead of grounded in immeasurable, soulful qualities.

We are not born with an ego. Infants have no sense of self; rather, they feel oneness with their mother and other primary caregivers. It isn't until the ego begins to develop at around age two that a child experiences themself as a separate being. We create a healthy ego if we grow up feeling bonded to our caregivers and feel loved and secure. If our home life is chaotic, if we experience trauma, and if we don't feel loved or attached to caregivers, we develop unhealthy egos. The ego is trying to protect us and will shut off parts of ourselves to shield us against future hurts. It gives us a sense of security and safety. Unless we recognize and heal our early wounds, our adaptive fear-based behaviors can cause deep emotional pain and a lack of self-love and connection. Our egos are not all healthy or unhealthy but usually a combination of both. By watching our reactions to daily situations, we'll learn to quickly recognize unhealthy patterns instead of being controlled by them.

The ego functions when we're absorbed in stories of the past and future but not when our attention is focused on the present moment. Clinging to attachments, outcomes, people, and situations keeps the ego engaged, and the attachment causes us suffering. Since the ego needs to struggle to survive, suffering dissolves when we quit struggling. When we let go of how we think life should be, we observe life as it is.

As Buddha said, "Attachment is the root of all suffering; detach from it and find inner peace."

The following statements show that the ego exhibits attitudes that operate from either a healthy or unhealthy ego. As you read them, do you understand how our response to situations determines the health of our ego? As we dispassionately view our ego's reactions to events, we learn to observe whether we dwell in equanimity or uneasiness.

- Your parents gave you a check for your birthday, and you thought it wasn't enough. You're complaining to friends that your parents are cheap.
- You think your partner drinks too much and you keep asking them to change their behavior and tell them you'll leave if they don't.
- You're in traffic, and the car in front of you slams on the brakes. You blow your horn and yell profanities.
- A friend criticizes how your jeans fit, and you didn't take it personally.
- You try to learn how to play the piano, and you can't quickly master the piece you are working on, but you keep trying.

- You were expecting an award at work and didn't get it, but you were happy for the person who did.
- Your friend is voting for someone you believe is corrupt, but you try to understand their point of view.

The ego is at play in all these scenarios. The first three are examples of an unhealthy ego exhibiting ungrateful, controlling, and aggressive behaviors. The last four are examples of a healthy ego, exhibiting confidence, persistence, kindness, and understanding behaviors.

Please resist the impulse to judge the ego as good or bad. Problematic issues arise when we're lost in thinking about the past or future and are unaware that the ego is in control. Once we learn to observe our ego in action, we can choose to shift our attention to the present, where the ego doesn't exist. An integral part of awakening is to become aware of your ego characteristics because, without awareness, you'll be controlled by unexamined thoughts and behavior patterns. As you become more mindful of the traits you exhibit, you will spend less time controlled by unconscious emotional reactions.

An Unhealthy Ego = An Ego Unchecked

The unhealthy ego uses fear to keep us dwelling on problems that aren't real or have no solution. The wounded ego seeks external valuation and tends to strive for perfection. Someone with an unhealthy ego is usually controlled by fear and anxiety, has limiting beliefs, and is inclined to react with frustration, defensiveness, and anger. They are unable to problem-solve constructively and gravitate toward what is comfortable. The toxic, erroneous beliefs and conditioned behavior patterns of the ego trigger us to react in unproductive ways. People with unhealthy egos have insecurities hidden from themselves and perhaps from others as well.

I'm sure most of us can identify with many of the unhealthy personality traits that have played out during different phases of our lives. Whenever you dispassionately observe your behavior, you will find many of these characteristics have been operating for decades. Some behaviors and emotions manifest boldly in your personality, while others are subtle, even elusive, but still disrupt your inner peace.

You start to recognize behaviors exhibiting ego weaknesses that prevent you from feeling fully alive and experiencing a sense of peace. As you begin to watch your behaviors, you must not judge yourself; simply observe your interactions. You will witness the qualities you want to release and those you want to nurture. When are you being manipulative, rigid, or controlling? Do you ever find yourself judging and being critical, even if you are not doing it face-to-face, but as your inner dialogue? Is seeking approval from others important to you? Ego weaknesses, such as taking things personally, blaming others, or using anger to control people, derail the ability to experience life in the moment. But as you grow in awareness, you'll experience a new sense of freedom as you learn how to release unhealthy ego traits rooted in fear, negativity, and toxic thinking patterns. Unless you become aware of your ego's characteristics, they'll most certainly control you.

A Healthy Ego = An Ego in Check

The healthy ego helps us cope with life's difficulties and finds solutions to challenging situations. A person with a healthy ego has a mature personality and is inclined to be optimistic. They are generally authentic, flexible, and not overwhelmed by stressful situations. Compassionate, kind, and curious, a person with a healthy ego can easily give and receive love. They've been schooled in emotional intelligence and have healthy boundaries. When a triggering situation presents itself, a person who has clarity about their ego strengths and weaknesses can recognize their trigger and handle the situation with an appropriate response instead of an emotional reaction. They don't take things personally and can easily embrace different perspectives. When inevitable struggles and tragedies enter their lives, these strengths provide resilience to navigate rocky waters.

Do you identify with the healthy aspects of your ego? When people have problems, instead of trying to fix the issue, do you wait for them to ask for help? Are you comfortable admitting when you are wrong? Do you get curious when you make mistakes and think about other ways the situation could have been handled? Does the voice inside your head tell you that you are enough, you are worthy, and you are resilient?

For healthy ego characteristics, refer to page 77, and for unhealthy ego characteristics, refer to page 76.

How to Distance from Unhealthy Ego Characteristics

When you were young, you might have had internal messaging programmed into your subconscious mind, resulting in unhealthy ego characteristics. Let's look at some ways to shift from ego behaviors and beliefs that don't serve you to healthier behaviors. As we awaken from being lost in thought, it's enormously helpful not to take things personally. Examining our unhealthy programming while taking things personally will only make us self-critical.

Remember, we all have a combination of healthy and unhealthy ego characteristics. You are not alone in exhibiting behaviors that can be considered personality flaws. Feeling shame about your perceived shortcomings won't bring healing. Develop these two beneficial character strengths when you observe your behavior: curiosity and humor. If you get curious about why you've behaved in a certain way, you'll gain insight into why you behaved that way instead of judging and reprimanding yourself. And inviting humor to accompany your awakening journey will elicit a light-hearted buoyancy.

The key to recognizing and unraveling the thoughts and behaviors that hijack our peace and happiness is to become the Watchful Observer, fully explored in Trail Marker 4. We can distance ourselves from our unhealthy ego characteristics simply by being vigilant and dispassionately watching how we interact with the world. With practice, we learn a lot from our observations, the behaviors aligned with love that open our hearts and those that are reactions from a place of fear.

The Essence of the Soulful Self

Ego characteristics can also easily overshadow our soulful essence. The ego is a result of being identified with thoughts and feelings, both of which are fleeting. Our soulful essence lives in the quiet spaciousness where thoughts and feelings float by.

The soul is *eternally* being. Metaphorically, God is the sun, and we are the sun's rays. Spiritually, the soul is the eternal self that is pure consciousness; it is not born and does not die. People in touch with their soulful selves are deep thinkers, curious, empathetic, and self-reflective. They often exude a childlike innocence and a sense of humor. They also maintain equanimity, exhibiting an inner peace that is palpable. A soulful person knows their shortcomings and is patient and nonjudgmental about other's shortcomings. As a person awakens, they recognize divinity in everyone and everything. Conscious of their interconnectivity, they're no longer self-centered or self-absorbed. The soulful person doesn't cling to a vision of how things are "supposed to be" and responds to life as it unfolds. No longer on an emotional rollercoaster, they have a strong sense of being grounded and present. Soulful people are often leaders and teachers who help others gain freedom from unnecessary suffering.

Qualities that align with the soulful person include awareness ~ compassion ~ truth ~ love ~ forgiveness ~ authenticity ~ patience ~ peace ~ kindness ~ acceptance and joy. Your work will fine-tune your ability to recognize when you are consumed by ego consciousness and then use the tools in *Roadmap to Ease* to align with divinity. With continued practice, you will experience and exude the qualities listed above.

Take a Sacred Pause

How does one recognize their soulful self and let the light of divine energy move through them? When you shift your awareness away from thoughts in the mind to sensations in the body, you create a sacred pause, an opportunity to experience spaciousness and connect to your divine self. You can do this any time, but it's especially treasured when you're rushed, stressed, or overwhelmed. Simply slow down and take a deep breath. Let's practice. Stop reading or listening, and take several slow, deep breaths. Pay attention to your breath moving through your body and the sensations in the body. How did it feel?

This simple practice can shift your focus from the mind into the body and the present moment. Here, you can break cycles of frenetic energy by simply entering stillness. Just know that when you move into stillness, anxiety may grab your attention. When it does, notice the feelings and breathe into them. With practice, entering spaciousness will become familiar and comforting for you.

Another way to create a sacred pause is to take a break and go outside for a walk, even if only for a few minutes. Observe nature. Watch a flock of birds fly overhead, gaze at dancing clouds, or feel the breeze on your face. Bring your attention to your sensations and the sounds and smells around you.

Where Happiness Resides

We are happy when we align with our divinity and are connected to our soulful, creative selves. We experience joy inside, independent of external attachments or desires. Happiness isn't something we achieve; it's a state of being. When absorbed in unhealthy ego qualities, we feel separate and alone. When we experience our oneness, we bask in happiness and freedom.

What We Think Will Make Us Happy

When asked what would make them happy, people usually answer fame, beauty, material possessions, power, or wealth. It is easy to imagine that being a famous singer, governor, supermodel, or winning the lottery will bring happiness. Still, we have no idea if any of these things would bring joy – do we? Assuming they are a first-class ticket to happiness is just a story someone has constructed. Continually fanaticizing about a life one doesn't have results in living in the future. You may feel confident that you'll be happy when you achieve external things, but really, you're just postponing happiness as you live with a nagging desire for what you don't have.

Aspiring to be beautiful is a poignant example of this nagging desire. Influenced by the media's strict standards for beauty, many people try to achieve a more desirable look. Many women base their body image – how they think and feel about themselves physically and how they believe others see them – on images of women in magazines and on the Internet. From the days of Twiggy until only recently, supermodels have been pencil-thin. How many eating disorders develop because a woman or young girl wants the body of a Photoshopped supermodel? Men also deal with image issues, desiring six-pack abs, muscular arms, and a full head of hair.

When self-esteem comes from physical appearance, aging can also be challenging. How much mental energy is spent thinking about losing weight, getting rid of cellulite, eliminating wrinkles, or going bald? How often do people waste money and time on failed diets, unused gym memberships, and exercise equipment? How many closets are filled with multiple sizes of clothes in case enough weight is lost for a smaller size? The truth about a perfect body is that even the people you and I perceive as having the 'ideal body' may very well be insecure about their body image.

It's not wrong to desire material possessions or to work hard to become a famous actor or actress; just don't postpone your happiness until you achieve your desires. The more you appreciate what you already have instead of thinking about what you don't have, the happier you'll be.

Don't let your mantra be "if only." "If only I had more money." "If only I had the leading role." "If only I had a meaningful relationship." Waiting for a desired outcome that may never arrive is a set-up for dissatisfaction.

As Buddha said, "Happiness will never come to those who fail to appreciate what they already have."

Enjoy the journey. While you work toward achieving what you desire, learn to engage in things that make you happy in the present moment. Savor what you have and be grateful for what you might be taking for granted. Remember to question the motives behind your desires. Are they mere ego distractions, or are they in attunement with your soulful life?

What Will Really Make Us Happy?

Happiness studies reveal that people generally want the same things, but the things they want are not necessarily the things they pursue. What are the things that, if we seek, we'd be happy? Let's ask ourselves, "Are we surviving or thriving?" Our survival needs are food, water, clothing, and shelter. After our survival needs are met, we need safety and security, which are our basic needs. The third and fourth needs are psychological: a sense of connection, being part of a community, and a sense of self-worth and self-esteem. The first four needs can hijack our happiness when they go unmet.

The longer a need goes unsatisfied, the stronger it gets. For instance, if I have low self-esteem and lack a feeling of self-worth, I can spend a lifetime trying to heal my soul holes by seeking remedies outside myself, such as people-pleasing, pursuing material desires, or abusing substances.

Once our survival and basic needs are met, we aspire to discover and develop our abilities and talents. The fifth human need is our growing edge, where we move beyond who we are and engage in becoming the best version of ourselves. Recognizable qualities of a self-aware person include independence, creativity, originality, and courage. Their curiosity about the meaning and purpose of life is explored, and as they awaken, feelings of awe, wonder, and sustained happiness are experienced.

Life can always throw us a curveball, and inevitably, we will experience challenging and devastating times, hard losses, and grieving cycles. From ashes, we can rise again. As we continue engaging in practices that expand our awareness, unhealthy ego traits are replaced by healthy ego traits. Exploration of the inner life fosters soulful quality growth, creating a happy, aware, interconnected life absorbed in the divine flow.

What Does Regret Have to Do with Happiness?

Universally, two questions at life's end seem to surface: Am I loved? and, Have I loved well? I think it's safe to say that on your deathbed, you likely won't be thinking about the amount of money in your bank account, the expensive car in the garage, linens you didn't change, or errands you didn't run. But many people do express other consistent regrets at the end of their lives. Many wished they had cared more about their bodies and less about what others thought. They wished they had traveled more and, when home, that they had spent more time with friends. They wished they had listened more and talked less.

And when it was the right time to talk, they regretted not saying "I love you" much more often or speaking their mind rather than holding back and harboring resentments. They regretted not pursuing more dreams and taking more chances. They wished they had been gentler with themselves and others. As you can see, their regrets had more to do with people and experiences, not possessions or status.

We all have an excellent opportunity to incorporate changes today to experience more peace, ease, and fulfillment. Please don't wait until the end of your life to take inventory of what you want and suffer remorse because it's too late. Make time now to do more of what lights you up so you can have a happy, creative, purpose-filled life without regret.

Here is a short exercise to assess whether you are doing the things that genuinely bring you joy. It will reveal areas of your life to reflect upon and question whether there are patterns and behaviors you need to change to mitigate regrets. You'll need a journal and a pen. Ponder the questions below. As you read them over, flash forward several decades from now and ask your future self, ideally, what your life would look like for you to feel enriched, happy, and fulfilled. What shifts might you make now to facilitate a life without regrets in the future? Write the questions that resonate with you in your journal, as well as the changes you want to make.

For example, "Do I make assumptions and not ask questions to determine if they are true?"

I make too many assumptions and regret it when I discover my assumptions are wrong. In the future, when I make assumptions, I will ask the person directly if my thinking is accurate. When we recognize incidences where we don't protect our best interests and make a simple shift to align with our soulful self, we are awakening.

Read the list below often and listen to which questions speak to you. If you want to shift a behavior that no longer serves you, write it down in your journal and do the exercise above. Doing this will give you valuable information about where you are stuck, help you articulate the changes you can make, and keep you on the road to a regret-free life.

- Do I spend the right amount of time with my friends and family?
- Am I kind and considerate?
- Do I do what is expected of me, or do I foster the things that are important to me?
- Is work consuming my life?
- Do I cultivate interests that bring me joy?

- Do I embrace humor and fun?
- Do I give back to make the world a better place?
- Do I worry too much?
- Do I make assumptions and don't ask questions to find out if they are true?
- Are there friends I've lost touch with that I miss?
- Do I listen to my instincts?
- Do I sweat the small stuff?
- Are there conflicts I am harboring that need addressing?
- Are my spending and savings habits where I want them to be?
- Do I take life too seriously?
- Do I take things personally?

Embrace the Adventure!

Heraclitus, the ancient Greek philosopher, said, "The only thing constant is change."

We can either get jiggy with change or fight it. Fighting 'what is' creates suffering. Since my mission in writing *Roadmap to Ease* is to teach you how to alleviate suffering's pitfalls, I invite you to read it – to experience it – with a mindset that makes room for change. While change may not be easy, taking this path to relax into your essence is such a worthy pursuit. The gifts you find along the path will be priceless – happiness, peace, freedom, and joy! Insights will illuminate your way like fireflies against a coal-black sky.

I invite you to commit to embracing curiosity and humor. Open your heart as you learn to observe daily life experiences without judgment or expectation and gain the wisdom their gleanings have to offer. Are you ready to embark on this extraordinary adventure and navigate the spiral path to enlightenment? OK then, let's go!

Simple Mindfulness Shifts

Pay attention to the daily activities you do without thought, like grabbing your phone to check text messages, going to the fridge when you aren't hungry, looking for something but forgetting what it is, and scrolling mindlessly through social media.

Observe when you feel relaxed and when you don't and notice what you're doing at the time.

Recognize when you are seeking distractions or doing something to "feel good." Are you looking to fulfill a need?

Why Wake Up?

> "Nothing can harm you as much as your own thoughts unguarded."
>
> *– Buddha*

What Preoccupies Your Mind?

Ask yourself, "When I draw my final breath, will I be at peace with my life choices, or will I be burdened with regrets? Will I have embraced a life of joy, or will I have suffered unnecessarily during life's unfolding events?"

The choices you make today hold the key to these answers. By simply observing your day-to-day activities, you can unlock a path of inner growth, alleviate unnecessary suffering, and lead a happier life.

Learning to observe your reactions to everyday situations will be your compass as you connect with a deeper awareness within and cultivate a calm mind – all from the comfort of your own home. My purpose in writing *Roadmap to Ease* is to teach you how to observe the way you react to your thoughts and feelings, how to nurture self-love, heal your emotional wounds, fill your heart with gratitude, and awaken to your divine nature.

I understand this may seem like a daunting task! But trust me, it's more of a promise. My goal is to empower you to be your own spiritual guide. And you won't need to go on a two-week meditation retreat, end your relationship, wait until your kids are grown, or postpone awakening until retirement. You can begin NOW.

And what about now? Is your life *now* an inspired masterpiece born from a divine spark or a labored effort to yield a harvest planted in nearly barren soil? Or is it a combination? Choices you make in the present moment become the opus of your life because NOW is the only moment in which you live. Does any of the following ring true for you? It certainly does for me. Too often, you squander vital energy as you spend precious time thinking about the past or fanaticizing about the future. You find yourself following trails of made-up stories that swirl in the mind when you fail to ask whether your perceptions are accurate. And then, you project. You obsess. Judge. Blame. Resist. Make excuses. Procrastinate. Do you ever strive for perfection and question your worthiness, focusing on what you don't have instead of what you do? Bargaining for approval – from parents, employers, teachers, partners, and most importantly from yourself has become the norm. Do you compare yourself to others and doubt your brilliance? Do you find yourself coveting what others have, confident that if you had what they did – life partner, wealth, job, or fit body – surely then you'd finally be happy?

You lacerate your soul with negative self-talk: "That was so stupid!" "What was I thinking?" "What a big mouth!" "Why did I say that?"

If any of this rings true, know you are not alone. Our self-talk most likely isn't that dissimilar from one another. Devastation and exhaustion from addictions, trauma, and significant loss are experiences that reflect our shared humanity. The mind's monologue and endless chatter may paint distinct scenes, but we each have recognizable storylines.

Let's have an honest discussion about these behaviors, how they may contribute to living unconsciously, without awareness, and what the ramifications in daily life look like. To begin with, they negatively affect your relationship with your children, parents, partners, and friends, your spiritual life, and even your relationship with food. They are the reason you hide your vulnerability or tuck your head into your shell when you feel afraid to speak from the heart. They cause you to dance around an issue so you don't hurt someone's feelings or be judged as 'too much.'

I've done *all* these things for decades and know I am not alone. I also know that the pitfalls of suffering caused by these behaviors veil the light of our true luminous being within. So, I will accompany you as you make this journey of discovery, awe, simplicity, and celebration that will reveal your true essence. Together, we'll approach this adventure with humor, curiosity, and a humble spirit as you learn shifts that, when practiced, awaken you to the present moment. You'll dig into the core of what is raw, authentic, and eternal to shed self-judgment and unchallenged beliefs. In these ways, you'll define what you really want, possibly discovering you already have it. *The challenge is to get curious about what makes you tick.* As you do, little by little, you will free yourself from weighty stories that bog down your life – a life created by experiences of your unique socialization process.

You'll come to understand how you developed opinions and judgments about your life stories, which gave them meaning, and then judged others based on these perceptions. For many of us, this rote behavior can become a vicious cycle of projection! For example, I grew up in a home with a mother who believed there was no reason for anyone to be homeless. Whenever she saw a homeless person, she'd say, "The grocery store always has a help-wanted sign. Why don't those people get a job?"

My young mind hadn't yet formed an opinion about homeless people; I didn't even know what homeless meant. But over time, consciously or subconsciously, I accepted this same belief. My mom's story about homeless people became my story, too. Later in life, during my personal journey toward enlightenment, I learned how to be the Watchful Observer and witnessed my thoughts and stories from a distance. With this awareness, I disengaged from my reactionary self and then experienced a shift. I no longer thought, *"Why don't they get a job?"* whenever I saw a homeless person. As I gained distance from this adopted, learned belief about homeless people, I realized I had no judgment about them, only compassion.

Maybe you've already had the experience of hearing yourself parrot a judgment you adopted in youth, only to realize it isn't what you believed in your heart. As you work through the exercises in *Roadmap to Ease*, you'll extract rich nutrients from *your* life stories (birth to the present), weeding out whatever stunts your spiritual development. You will also use practices that teach you how to deal with an unruly mind and how to recognize deeply suppressed feelings. Collectively, these practices can be your stepping stones to enlightened consciousness. Choosing to bravely follow them will lead you toward what makes your heart sing and puts a smile on your face, to a quiet place within where you can let kindness and love expand your heart. This ever-present choice is yours to make.

Albert Einstein said, "There are only two ways to live your life. One is as though nothing is a miracle. The other is as though everything is a miracle."

I choose to believe that everything is a miracle and that life is magical, although sometimes difficult, too.

As you courageously walk this path to enlightenment, you will begin to see that the ego, your self-concept, has eclipsed your divinity. And as you peel away the layers of who you perceived yourself to be, which obscured access to your limitless self, you will experience greater ease in your body and recognize a vast, spacious feeling within and without. You will become braver and more authentic and compassionate toward yourself and others. You will release strong judgments and expectations about how people are supposed to behave or how events should unfold. When you choose levity over unnecessary seriousness, you'll find that you exude a buoyancy and joy that is noticeably intriguing. And when you do experience turbulent feelings, instead of running from them or masking them, you can learn to give them attention, feel them fully, and let the energy move through your body.

Life is like a kaleidoscope. When I look through one, I see the scene as if it were a photograph. But when I turn the kaleidoscope just one degree – only one little shift – an entirely distinct perspective comes into my view. All too often, it can feel like life is happening *to* you. The truth is that you are co-creating life with the eternal divine source from which you are indivisible. You can always *choose* when it's time to turn the kaleidoscope.

What Is Enlightenment?

Well, first, let's imagine it's lunchtime in a bustling city. You're watching people swiftly move along the sidewalk. Some people dart into cafes, and others walk dogs. Many talk on cell phones, appearing to be a million miles from any awareness of the pavement beneath their feet. It's as though each person's arms and legs are attached to strings. Like Pinocchio, Mister Geppetto's puppet, they do not control their own movements. So, what is? The subconscious mind pulls the strings, where the stored beliefs, memories, feelings, habits, and behavior patterns control their actions.

Scenes like the one I described here mimic the reality of life for most people. Too often, they live this way, lost in the mind's chatter, having internal dialogues that cloud their experience of present moments.

> "I need to buy two potatoes for dinner tonight."
> "Damn, I forgot to make a doctor's appointment."
> "I wonder if the picnic will be rained out this weekend."

Even the people walking side by side conversing are only half listening to each other. As one person talks, the other rehearses what they will say next, anxiously awaiting their turn to speak.

However, some individuals in the bustling city scene have liberated themselves from conditioned behaviors. They experience the sun's warmth on their face, listen to the sound of a passing ambulance screech, feel a breeze blow wisps of their hair, and notice their stomach growling from emptiness. *Although the voice in their head still drones on in the background, their attention is in the present moment.*

We don't become enlightened; enlightenment is a state of being. Enlightenment is awareness itself, recognizing the nature of its being. From this enlightened or pure consciousness, we no longer experience life solely through the ego lens of thoughts, feelings, perceptions, and beliefs. The content of each experience is now viewed in awareness. We recognize what is transitory and, in the quiet mind, watch the comings and goings of thoughts and emotions, offering no resistance to the storylines marching through the mind. Without resistance, the little "i," the ego, recedes, and what becomes known is the "I AM," the spacious infinite awareness. Enlightened consciousness, awareness without a sense of self, can only be experienced in the NOW.

The path to enlightenment can be likened to an artichoke bud, the heart representing pure consciousness and the petals representing the layers of the ego made up of judgment, opinions, dogma, and expectation. Though pure consciousness is ever present, it is revealed only when one peels back the outer petals of illusionary ego consciousness to find that the 'heart' was there all along. This state of enlightenment exists within everyone, but ego eclipses ever-present awareness.

Rumi eloquently expresses the nature of enlightenment, "You are not a drop in the ocean; you are the entire ocean in a drop."

When you identify with the ego, you experience yourself as a drop within the ocean, alone in its vastness. When you are enlightened, you experience being a drop in the ocean *and* the entire ocean. When you shift from the ego and the individual limited sense of self to the conscious, Watchful Observer, you awaken.

This journey is a uniquely individual experience. Some people choose a life of renunciation to find enlightenment. Others become devotees of spiritual teachers, dedicating their lives to the path of enlightenment. Still others, experiencing deep depression, with no prior spiritual leanings, become enlightened instantly. Here's the excellent news: While walking the path of enlightenment, one doesn't have to renunciate and shed all earthly possessions, sit countless hours in the lotus position, or recite mantras thousands of times.

Lao Tzu said, "Knowing others is wisdom. Knowing yourself is enlightenment."

As you watch yourself with awareness, distanced from the mind's monologue, you will awaken. As you observe moments of daily life filled with beliefs, thoughts, actions, emotions, and events, each will offer profound insights to facilitate your spiritual growth.

A Gradual Awakening

The journey to enlightenment doesn't generally progress on a linear path but rather along a constantly changing spiral course. It shows itself when you think you've outgrown an unhealthy behavior only to have the behavior reappear. No worries. Awareness does not judge. You're always on this path, even when darkness envelops you or you are unaware that a path even exists. So, when your attention returns to awareness in the present moment, you will recognize the path you are on.

And as you awaken, you will see that the path leads away from self-centered pursuits toward a more heart-centered life. While the ego will still be a motivating factor in your decision-making, a purpose greater than yourself takes root. It can feel like you have taken two steps forward and one step back. As you continue to negotiate the challenges and lessons of everyday life and learn from its teachings, you will realize that the journey to awakening is a vast, multifaceted experience in which your patience grows.

Curiosity about why you do what you do, accompanied by a sense of humor, are great companions on the awakening journey. Humor helps you not take things personally and to have some fun as you navigate the path to greater freedom. Mindfulness and curiosity help you notice when you're in the ego's grasp, without distance from thoughts, beliefs, emotions, and behaviors. Your awareness increases each time you see that you're immersed in storylines of past and future projections. When you practice expanding awareness, you shift from the confines of the mind into the spaciousness of pure consciousness. When meditating or wandering in nature, you may enter a state of "no mind," an infinite spaciousness that contains all that is, where you are bathed in peace and happiness, where you *are* peace and happiness.

Certain life situations bring continual challenges, such as the death of a loved one, a health crisis, or a financial disaster. Having access to spacious awareness can offer respite. Less challenging situations, such as a fight with a friend, your child's tantrum, or a nasty comment on a social media feed, offer endless opportunities to observe your reactions, let feelings move through you, and breathe into inner peace as the experience unfolds.

With other life situations, it feels as though gale-force winds whip up, catching you in the tornadic activity of the ego's outburst. You may find yourself screaming into the phone at an annoying, robotic customer service representative, losing patience with an aging parent, or judging a mother feeding candy and soda to her child for lunch. You know you are waking up when you observe each moment unfold and choose not to react with anger, frustration, and harsh judgment. Instead, you pause to breathe and experience feelings moving through you.

When you no longer believe or are attached to ranting phrases that enter your mind like, "I'm unworthy," "I am too fat," or "I'll never have enough money," you are awakening.

When your inner dialogue utters judgments of others such as, "They are idiots," "What a loser," or "Their outfit looks hideous," and you simply shift into observing your thoughts without judgment, you are awakening. You are awareness watching the theatrics of a reactive ego.

Buddha said, "Every morning we are born again. What we do today is what matters most."

We can't say with certainty we'll live through the day. What we do NOW matters most. You can choose to let thoughts and stories about your past reside in your mind, dictating your future, or you can choose to let them melt like snowflakes warmed by the sun. You can also ritualistically give death to attachments and weighty stories from your past and enter the present moment. Would you like to choose to be part of the tribe of awakened souls and divine beings that we truly are? I would – join me!

Know What Your Brain Does So It Won't Trip You Up

Be Aware – Don't Stumble

A giant step toward becoming happy and feeling at ease is understanding that some of life's biggest obstacles occur because of how the mind is wired and the nature of its thoughts. When you understand the constraints of human biology and learn how to distance yourself from your thoughts through meditation and mindfulness, you can gain freedom from unnecessary suffering.

When following *Roadmap to Ease*, it's important to remember there are obstacles that can sabotage your well-being and shroud your happiness. Two giant boulders that block our access to peace and happiness often go unrecognized for a lifetime, but no longer! The first is not having the information about how your brain is wired and how that wiring can trip you up. The second is not fully understanding the nature and power of subconscious programming and how thoughts and beliefs can dictate habitual behaviors. I'll discuss both obstacles here, and you'll learn how to gain freedom from being controlled by programming in later chapters.

Although the terms brain and mind are often used interchangeably, they differ. The brain is a physical object that can be touched, whereas the mind is a function of electrical brain activity and can't be touched. Amazingly, we can create structural change in our brains by using the thoughts in our minds.

The brain is a very busy organ, mysterious and grand in its design, and said to be the most complex object in the universe. It is our central computer that is responsible for automatic behaviors such as heartbeat and temperature control, as well as regulating motor, organ, and speech functions. The brain also enables thoughts, decisions, memories, and emotions. The brain's neurons (nerve cells) exchange information with the rest of the body's nervous system through the spinal cord, which goes from the brain down through the back. The nervous system network is a highway of chemical and electrical impulses carrying messages back and forth from the brain to different parts of the body.

It's not necessary to know everything about the workings of your brain to understand how its wiring can trip you up. Just know that you can still avoid feeling controlled by its very efficient central computer operating on software installed without your awareness. Understanding the constraints of human biology and observing your reactions to daily life situations will open you to experience a newfound state of relaxation as your attention moves from the density of thoughts into spacious awareness.

For easy reference, here is a list of the brain functions and energetic activities of the mind that can trip you up and, at times, result in repetitious and reactionary behavior. *So re-read this section whenever you feel stuck, reactive, or behave in ways you don't understand.* You will learn to recognize when your brain is functioning on autopilot. This awareness will give you a better understanding of your mysterious brain, which informs your body's responses so as not to be ruled by them. By practicing observation, simple mindfulness shifts, meditations, and pondering questions offered in this book, you will awaken.

The Conscious Mind

When deciding what job offer to take or planning your summer vacation, what part of the mind are you using? It's the conscious part of the brain immediately behind the forehead, known as the prefrontal cortex, that is responsible for higher-level thinking. This includes critical thinking, impulse control, managing emotional responses, short-term memory, language, decision-making, and creativity. The conscious mind receives messages from the senses, oversees planning, and knows what we want to do in life. This part of the mind changes easily. Neuroscientists believe the conscious mind is engaged 5% of the time.

The Subconscious Mind

The subconscious mind is in the brain's subcortical area (beneath the cortex and deep within the brain), functioning as a cloud storage memory bank. Responsible for memories and beliefs, it stores and retrieves data and *records all our experiences, both positive and negative.* The subconscious mind always operates, tending to automatic functions such as breathing, heartbeat, and temperature, and takes over when the conscious mind is lost in thought. It continually makes sense of information, searching its database to find repetitive actions that it turns into automatic movements. For example, when we first learn to drive a car, we must be fully aware of all the actions we must perform to operate the car correctly. This engages the conscious mind. Then, to help us become more efficient, the subconscious mind records all those actions, and a habit is formed so we can perform repetitive tasks, like driving, without relying on the conscious mind.

The subconscious mind operates efficiently but not always accurately, as does the conscious mind. Since the subconscious mind can't reason, it doesn't judge, think, or change information easily. It obeys commands from the conscious mind and is ruled by instinct and learned responses. Subconscious brain activity operates habitually – about 95% of the time – sorting information with lightning speed compared to the slowly operating conscious mind. This means that our actions happen on autopilot 95% of the time.

The Amygdala and Hippocampus

The limbic brain (or mammalian brain) plays a role in regulating emotional responses and the storage of memories. It houses the amygdala and hippocampus. The hippocampus is involved in memory encoding, learning, and emotional behavior and regulates the stress response. The amygdala is best known for its fight, flight, or freeze response when there is a perceived threat and is involved in emotional responses such as fear, anger, anxiety, and pleasure. When a stressful event occurs, the amygdala sends a distress response to the hippo-campus, which in turn sends a signal to the adrenal glands. The adrenal glands pump adrenaline into the bloodstream, causing the heart to beat faster, which starts a cascading ef-fect, resulting in more energy being pumped through the body so it can respond to the danger at hand. When the threat has subsided, the frontal lobe signals to the amygdala there is no longer danger. When a person has endured significant trauma, the frontal lobe can fail to shut down the amygdala's survival response, causing anxious symptoms that will wear you down over time. Breathing exercises and physical exercises can help re-regulate the amygdala.

Dopamine

Dopamine, a chemical produced in the brain, is a neurotrans-mitter responsible for brain functions that include thinking, sleeping, movement, paying attention, and motivation. Its most important function, for this discussion, is that it plays a sig-nificant role in reward-motivated behavior. It sets up the desire to seek and get a reward, which is explained at length at the end of this chapter.

Conformity Bias

Do you find yourself caring what other people think about you? Do you desire to be accepted by your tribe? Have you ever had a different opinion than a group of peers but didn't speak up because you didn't want to rock the boat or feel judged? Why do many of us answer "yes" to these questions? It's because of conformity bias, a companion to the brain's fight, flight or freeze response.

Conformity bias, linked to two brain regions, is the tendency to change one's beliefs and behaviors to align with what we perceive our peers believe to belong and feel accepted. This bias has its roots in primal behavior. Our tribal ancestors' survival depended upon not doing something that went against what the majority of leaders believed. Consequently, they'd modify their behavior to fit in. They couldn't risk being ostracized by the tribe, which meant certain death because anyone banned from the tribe could not survive alone in nature.

Negativity Bias

Isn't it true that you can get hundreds of "likes" and positive comments on social media, but if you get one negative comment, that is where you put your focus? Why is this true for so many people? Why do we give more focus to negative attention than to positive attention? It's called negativity bias. Again, it goes back to our wiring for self-preservation to ensure we remain vigilant to danger in our environment. That pesky lion could jump out anytime and end our lives, so we're on high alert, expecting the worst. Without practicing mindfulness and attention shifts, we'll be influenced by negative, undisciplined thoughts and emotions more than positive ones, affecting our mood, self-talk, and how we interact with people.

Why the Brain Needs to Be Rewired

The human brain has developed over time yet still has wiring that was necessary for survival in primitive societies. The brain's hardwiring with the fight, flight, or freeze response guaranteed our survival then, but in today's times, it creates behaviors that are not always in our best interest. This simply means we still run on the same operating system needed to produce an adrenaline dump necessary to escape a hungry lion! But this operating system *can be* upgraded as you grow in awareness, and I will teach you how to do it.

When you learn to observe your subconscious repetitive behavior and come to understand why you do what you do, you can practice simple shifts you'll learn throughout this book and discover feelings of peace and ease multiplying.

Looking at how we grow up is helpful to grasp why we are reactive beings. Our primary experience as babies involves getting our needs met. We seek comfort and cry when hungry, have a wet diaper, or are in pain. We learn about the world through the senses. The needs of parents or caregivers are not even in the realm of an infant's comprehension. Then, around age three, we begin to realize that our behavior affects those around us. We start to examine situations, recognizing that impulsive behavior sometimes does not produce the desired outcome. We modify our pleasure-seeking behaviors as we become aware the world isn't all about us, and we start taking other people into consideration. Around age five, our moral compass begins to develop as we take on the morals of those around us: parents, siblings, caregivers, and teachers. This is how we develop the concept of right and wrong.

Because we learn from the people we've grown up and interacted with, we have adopted behaviors and life views based on the reactions and reflections of other people. All this learning is recorded by the subconscious mind, and by age seven, it is the program that sparks feelings, beliefs, emotions, and behaviors we run on for life, operating without our conscious awareness or input. Since the conscious mind is limited in the information it stores, it's often unaware of why you do what you do; therefore, most of the time, we operate on unconscious programming. For instance, someone may say something that stirs a profound emotional reaction within you that seems disproportionate to what was actually said. This happens when an encounter with someone restimulates a hurt from the past buried deep within the subconscious.

Even though you are a product of socialization and brain wiring, you *can* grow in awareness and recognize this kind of dynamic by practicing mindfulness and incorporating what science tells us about brain plasticity or neuroplasticity. In essence, neuroplasticity means that the brain has the capacity to continue to grow and change by forming new network connections. This means you don't have to remain hostage to a programmed mind.

In 1949, Donald Hebb discovered "Neurons that fire together wire together." Up until the 1970s, scientists believed that the brain was immutable after early childhood. But scientific advancements reveal we can rewire the brain. New findings in the field of neuroplasticity confirm that the brain grows and changes over a person's lifespan. Some leading neuroscientists now agree with what Buddhists have adhered to for thousands of years: the mind can be changed by training it.

How Do We Rewire the Brain?

To emerge from a life running on autopilot based on subconscious programming, we must remain conscious of our desire to reprogram the brain. We *decide to be aware* of our subconscious programming and stay alert to where our attention is. We also assure ourselves that we're willing to change. I know it can be challenging to let go of painful behaviors because a basic shared human need is certainty. Even when we know negative thought loops and limiting behavior patterns are detrimental, letting go of what is familiar and stepping into the unknown can be scary and make us feel vulnerable. It's important to remember that the subconscious records all experiences, both positive and negative. To reprogram limiting and negative subconscious beliefs, repetition is needed to rewire the brain's pathway. The deeper the belief is ingrained; the more repetition is necessary for change to occur over time. Repetition is the golden ticket to brain rewiring. You can choose to do it joyously. Buddha said, "If you do what is good, keep repeating it and take pleasure in making it a habit. A good habit will cause nothing but joy."

The subconscious mind understands the language of imagery and emotions, so how do you use these to rewire your subconscious and change the default behavior patterns? Let's say you are terrified of public speaking because you believe you're a poor public speaker. When you try to speak to groups of people, your voice shakes, and your hands tremble. To overcome this limitation and rewire your belief, visualize yourself calmly walking on the stage and "feel" yourself get centered, looking into the eyes of your audience. "See" yourself standing confidently and effortlessly giving your speech. "Hear" your voice speaking with authority. To make the rewiring more potent, "feel" how present you are in your body and experience your breath filling your lungs, rhythmic and steady. "See" the participants clapping feverishly at the end of your speech and "feel" yourself soaking in their appreciation.

The subconscious mind doesn't know the difference between fantasy and reality. Visualizing and feeling an event happening is experienced by the subconscious in the same way as an actual event. Write the script you want your life to look like, then "see" and "feel" yourself doing it. In this example, you're rewiring a default pattern of behavior that elicits fear when you try to speak.

I'm sure you're asking, "But how do I rewire negative thought loops?" First, you identify the thoughts and feelings that elicit a negative reaction in you.

"I could never get a college degree."
"I will never lose weight."
"I don't have a creative bone in my body."

You change these thoughts in the same way you changed behavior. Remember, the part of the brain that processes emotion doesn't distinguish between real or imagined experiences. You can engage in the new experience and simply imagine how you will feel when you achieve the new behavior or life experience you desire. You need to have success and feel emotions associated with a triumphant experience to cement the new wiring.

Let's take the negative thought, "I will never lose weight." You repeatedly "see" yourself standing in a full-length mirror as the thinner you. You "hear" yourself ordering a meal full of healthy choices, and you "feel" yourself walking into a party wearing jeans that are the exact size you want to be. While forming these new habits, you need to engage your brain as well as supercharge your thoughts with emotional responses in your body; in other words, get excited!

The longer you've had a behavior, the more challenging it will be to change it. Be patient. Change won't happen overnight, but with perseverance, new habits will take hold. I suggest that rather than trying to change several negative behaviors at once, focus on one behavior at a time, listing the reasons why making the change is a worthy endeavor. I also suggest you make up mantras to counter repetitive negative thoughts and strengthen your desired behavior. If you are feeling depressed and want to be happier, your mantra could be, "I welcome happiness," or "I have everything I need to be happy." A subsequent new habit will form when you repeatedly think, feel, and behave in a way that aligns with your desired 'new' behavior.

There are several other ways to rewire your brain. Meditation has measurable effects on the brain. Scientists who study the correlation between meditation and neuroplasticity revealed that brain function in experienced meditators is positively affected in eight brain areas. This information is extremely encouraging because those of us raised in less-than-optimal circumstances, suffer from posttraumatic stress disorder, or have fed the brain a steady diet of negative thoughts can affect change in the brain with meditation.

You can foster your brain rewiring by incorporating new adventures into your daily routines. The brain stays active and healthy by forming new connections when it digests new information. Develop a curious nature and venture into the world of podcasts or learn a second language. Dive into creative endeavors like exploring the world of art and music. Walk in nature and let your being absorb the wonders of the universe. Keep a dream journal and learn how to interpret the mind's subconscious messages. Live with a heart of gratitude and frequently count your blessings. Surround yourself with positive and interesting people. And just for good measure, eat foods that supercharge the brain: green veggies, fatty fish, nuts, seeds, and berries.

Why You Need "Shifts" to Wake Up?

Throughout *Roadmap to Ease,* I introduce numerous 'shifts,' or mindfulness practices that enable you to recognize when you've become lost in thought or are wrestling with 'what is.' They essentially wake you up so you can identify repetitive thoughts and patterns and be freed from mind chatter. They also help you become aware of how often you over-complicate life, which results in unnecessary suffering. Through mindfulness, you will reestablish a connection to your divinity, inner rhythm, creativity, and sense of well-being.

The mind's narrative is typically about the past or future. No wonder we are kept from living in the present when life's constant attention grabs keep interrupting us. We're all easily distracted by the next shiny object. How often do we slip into the computer vortex that devours enormous chunks of time as we consume massive amounts of content? Studies vary about how often we touch our cell phones daily, but a glance around an airport terminal, restaurant, or lobby in a doctor's office gives a good indication – a lot!

Each time you look at your phone, you can become distracted, which can also take you into an endless loop of seeking. Have you ever wondered what happens physiologically when you are in this seeking mode? Or why some of us are addicted to checking e-mail, social media, texting, and searching for information online? I have, and the answer is *dopamine*. Our attention is hijacked by the brain's chemistry when we seek and get a reward. When we expect to receive a reward, whatever it may be, eating chocolate cake, listening to a favorite song, playing a video game, or reading a text message, dopamine – a type of neurotransmitter and chemical messenger – is released by the brain.

Dopamine is also involved with reinforcement. We may adjust our behavior to get more of whatever caused its release because – you guessed it – it made us feel good! We can end up chasing this "feel-good" sensation so much that it leads to a cycle of habitual use – even addiction, be it drugs, food, alcohol, compulsive shopping, sex, video games, gambling, social media – the list goes on and on. Although a dopamine rush makes us feel good, feeling powerless over substances or a behavior certainly doesn't make anyone feel happy, purposeful, or connected to their soulful self.

For many of us, the day begins with good intentions and a long to-do list. However, our attention wanders within a short time, and we find distractions to avoid what we want to accomplish. These distractions often include trips to the refrigerator when we're not hungry, the sudden need to search for a high-school friend we haven't seen for decades, an overwhelming desire to scour the Internet for the perfect black dress or to check airfares for a trip to Paris we can't afford. When in the search-

and-look-for-a-reward mode, we scramble for that dopamine hit. In this familiar scenario, we are caught in a search-and-reward loop, not in charge of creating our best life.

Programmers working for social media platforms designed tasks for users to perform while using their software with the intention of keeping them engaged. The "like" button was created so that each time we use it, it gives us a little dopamine hit that keeps us interacting with the site. Social media sites generate revenue from advertising, so the more users interact with a platform, the greater the opportunity to sell ads.

Folks, this struggle is real! Physically craving and endlessly seeking a dopamine rush keeps us in a reactive rather than receptive mode. We become like puppets with strings pulled by the addictive impulses in the brain. Many of us have experienced internal struggles when trying to lose weight, consume less social media, or reduce our alcohol consumption. It often feels like a fight between the forces of good and evil when we wrestle with habitual and addictive behaviors, attempting to exert our willpower to gain control over a negative mental dialogue and the craving for that dopamine hit.

We may even regularly make new goals: "I will lose 25 pounds," "I will stop buying lottery tickets," "I will quit texting while driving." Often, within a short time, we succumb to distractions and don't achieve the goal, continuing to be controlled by internal dialogue and reactionary behavior. Most people believe that simply exerting willpower to change their outer life will help them achieve weight loss, give them more focus, or be less restless, ultimately leading to true happiness. When we rely solely on exerting our willpower to change behaviors, we can create a cycle of unresolved inner conflict.

How do we create a more peaceful, self-determined, and spiritually aligned life during internal conflicted and counterproductive thought processes? How can we unravel this search-and-seek-reward cycle that traps us in a habitual trance? How do we break free of a life that lacks wonder, connection, and gratitude? *Roadmap to Ease* will answer these questions and so many more as you walk the path of awakening.

Following Roadmap to Ease

The word ease conjures up images of relaxing in a hammock, enjoying a good book, and feeling a general sense of well-being. We might think of ease as a life with less stress, more deep relationships, less drama and heartache, and more internal and external harmony and contentment. Concepts like satisfying work life, financial stability, and good health would most likely be discussed in a conversation about ease.

Don't mistake a life of ease for an easy life. Around each bend in the road, we're confronted with a new situation, some exhilarating and some distressing. Life is full of changes and challenges. A life of ease won't negate hard times, heartbreaking, or even horrific situations. So why follow the path to ease and choose to awaken? Because it's easy to get stagnant in life and remain stuck in patterns of behavior and insatiable wanting that rob us of joy and peace. Embarking on a journey of awakening shatters a fixed mindset and sets an energetic growth mindset in motion. Choosing a spiritual life path gives us direction and tools to work with and the insight to confront life's biggest challenges and glean the wisdom they have to offer. The lessons we've learned from our greatest struggles teach us the most. Overcoming our struggles might show us we have strength we never knew we had, and adversity might open our hearts to deep compassion for our fellow humans' difficulties. We may see that our priorities haven't aligned with a meaningful inner life, so we create a life of service based on the understanding we have garnered from adversity.

If you follow *Roadmap to Ease*, where will it take you? Don't expect to cross a finish line packed with adoring fans cheering you on, as there is no fixed destination. No award will be given to commemorate your accomplishments along the way, as an increased sense of peace and freedom are the prize. Don't worry about making right or wrong turns on this journey because there is no wrong way to do life. With practice, you'll gain distance from your thoughts, feelings, and beliefs. The less personal they become, the more you'll realize that a lot of the stress and suffering along life's journey is self-imposed. As your mindset shifts from focusing on an outer life to nurturing a rich inner life, you become more self-aware and self-accepting. Most likely, you'll find yourself projecting, judging, and expecting less; you won't be as reactive and won't feel like you're a victim of circumstance. If you have a general sense of malaise and dissatisfaction, it will wane. Learning to be gentle with yourself and getting curious about how you respond to daily life situations bathes you in ease and intrigue. You'll exude an attitude of gratitude, feel more relaxed, and have an overall sense of well-being.

As Khalil Gibran so eloquently said, "Your living is determined not so much by what life brings to you as by the attitude you bring to life; not so much by what happens to you as by the way your mind looks at what happens."

Trail Marker 3 takes you on a healing journey exercise, introducing you to the first shift, *Clear the Path to Enlightenment*. With the focused intention to release weighty baggage, you'll emerge buoyant and ready to embrace your awakened life fully.

I'll show you how to identify events in your life that have weighed you down, and then you will do an exercise to release them. I'll also guide you in the practice of recalling joyful and enriching times when you were growing up so that you can incorporate similar experiences into your spiritually aligned life. Grab a cup of tea, put on some comfy clothes, and get ready to release what weighs you down and embrace what lights you up.

Simple Mindfulness Shifts

When strong emotions surface during the day, feel where they are in your body and breathe into them until they pass.

When events happen, such as missing your ride or walking on the beach, label the feeling you are having, such as, "That's frustration" or "That's happiness." This practice will make you more aware of your feelings.

When listening to your inner dialogue, label the thought or story "that's in the past" or "that's in the future." This will help you be more aware when you're lost in thought and not in the present moment.

The First Shift
Clear the Path to Enlightenment

"You can choose to let thoughts and stories about your past reside in your head, dictating your future, or you can choose to let them melt like snowflakes warmed by the sun."

— e'Layne Kelley

Who is This Being Known as "Self"?

The physical self is composed of elements such as oxygen and nitrogen, as well as systems such as the digestive and nervous systems. The primary function of the nervous system is to send impulses to the brain, which tells the body what to do. In this way, the heart beats, temperature is regulated, and digestion takes place, all involuntarily, without one needing to think about it to make it happen. In addition to the physical self, there is a psychological, social, and spiritual self. Throughout *Roadmap to Ease*, I address the spiritual self, but in this chapter, I'll take you on a deep dive into the ways social influences shape, and continue to shape, our lives, sharing what I've learned by asking, "Who are we at birth and how do we grow up to become the intellectual, opinionated, and emotional beings we are as adults?"

Take a minute to close your eyes and visualize a newborn. An infant has no control over its physical actions; its movements are involuntary. It is sensitive to light and sound. Objects have no meaning to them, and actions have no consequences. Now think about what it would be like to be this baby, with no concept of right or wrong, no understanding of rules or social norms, and *no concept of existing as a separate being.* Is it difficult to imagine? Things that you and I have come to desire in adult life; money, material possessions, certainty, love, a profession, friendships, and travel, held no meaning when we were infants. The beliefs and passions for which we may be willing to give our life did not exist in our consciousness as newborns. This is because we are born a blank slate, and who we become results from our upbringing and the beliefs we adopt from life experiences.

Now, think of a toddler. When we observe children at this age, it's easy to see that they are sponges for learning, constantly exploring their surroundings through play and imagination. They have grown from being an infant who has no sense of self to a child becoming aware of their autonomy. They may develop fears and phobias and start to experience jealousy. The lines between real and make-believe may be blurred, but they are beginning to know *they are separate selves and that they can make choices.*

To understand how personality develops from infancy through adulthood and how it influences our daily lives, let's look at three influences that shape personality: heredity, environment, and situation. *Heredity* is the genetic makeup passed down from our biological parents, and it influences our physical appearance. It also appears to influence personality traits like openness, neuroticism, and extroversion. *Environment* refers to the surroundings and conditions where we grew up and where we currently live. This includes our home, school, workplace, and other places where we spend time. *Situation* refers to our circumstances and life experiences. This includes events such as the death of a loved one, parents divorcing, moving from town to town, people fighting in the home, and other traumatic events. Happy events are included as well.

We each grew up interacting with an array of caregivers who provided varying degrees of support. Parenting styles range from the 'helicopter parent' who hovers over their children to the parent who is emotionally unavailable to their children. These circumstances also influence the development of personality.

Each negative and positive life experience and how we respond to the experience shapes our personality. We are conscious of some of these experiences but have no memory of others. Either we were too young to remember, or the event was so traumatic the memory was blocked. Still, our beliefs, opinions, aspirations, and social behaviors are based on what we have internalized. For example, as I've told you, my father died when I was only one month old. When I was as young as two years old, my mom told me what it was like to lose her husband when she was so young. She also told me that she was under constant stress about money, wore black for two years, was skeletal from not eating, and was constantly sad and overwhelmed. So, you can see how my life situation was very much unlike that of a child raised with two happy parents. It's important to remember that because we have distinct upbringings by parents and caregivers with varying child-rearing styles, each individual's world will be recognizably different. Sometimes, an event, circumstance, or situation will bring some of this internal world to the surface, and we experience an opportunity for healing.

During my twenties, I had an experience that revealed why I struggled to form deep, intimate bonds. At the time, I was studying Transpersonal Counseling Psychology at John F. Kennedy University. During a Jungian dream workshop, participants sat in a circle, and I stood in the middle, sharing my previous night's dream. When I mentioned the image of the American flag, the professor asked me if the flag held significance in my life. I was swept away in a flood of emotion when I shared that I had the flag that was draped over my father's coffin. Since my dad died right after my birth, I was not conscious that his death had impacted my life. Ultimately, the dream work revealed my subconscious fear of abandonment, which sabotaged my ability to engage in deep, intimate relationships.

From Limitation to Liberation

Did you know that only a rope and a small stake in the ground can restrain an adult elephant? Even though it wouldn't have to pull hard on the rope to gain freedom, it doesn't make the effort. This is because when the elephant was a calf, a rope and stake were strong enough to keep it under control. It accepted the limitation and didn't attempt to gain freedom even though it grew older and stronger. The story of the elephant and the rope exemplifies what happens to humans who grow up with limitations.

As parents and caregivers, we need to be aware of the delicate balance between letting our kids roam and explore freely and keeping them safe. Ideally, children would follow their innate curiosity. They'd be allowed to investigate their surroundings, feel their feelings as they move through them, learn to comfort themselves and be permitted to learn by making mistakes. But often, parents pass their fears onto their children, limiting their children's experiences based on their own comfort level. What happens with the young elephant tethered to the rope is similar to what happens to humans during socialization. We learn which behaviors are acceptable and which are unacceptable, then we modify behaviors accordingly. Unless we have questioned why we do what we do, we're most likely limited in what we think we can do. When we believe we can't do something, we don't even try. Like the elephant, we are held by a stake and a rope. The stake is our subconscious programming, and the rope is woven of limited, unquestioned thoughts.

But fear not. You can learn to explore your personality and grow in awareness as the divine being you are. You can cultivate self-confidence, self-esteem, and curiosity. You can change your belief system, heal wounds, and expand beyond limited beliefs. Watching your words and actions without judgment gives you valuable insight into what makes you tick. Gaining this insight and the understanding you glean from simply observing your behavior and questioning your thoughts are essential keys to unlocking true freedom.

Unraveling Your Past

Understanding what makes us tick requires a time investment topped off with a heap of honest self-reflection and compassion. Because our adult behaviors and opinions reflect core beliefs we adopted during our childhood and early teen years, we want to bring to the surface those beliefs that don't serve us and then release them. For example, my mother compared my two brothers unmercifully. My younger brother, Scott, became the golden child. My older brother, Craig, was continually asked why he couldn't be more like Scott. From this comparison, Craig internalized that he wasn't good enough, wasn't lovable, and couldn't do anything right. In his teenage years, he became angry and pessimistic, turning to drugs and alcohol to mask his pain. Every conversation Craig engaged in quickly became about how mom didn't love him like she loved Scott. Feelings of inadequacy consumed Craig because he couldn't shake his life story. My brother, a beautiful, funny, loving young man, was unable to rewrite his life's story, and tragically, his pain led to an early death.

Sometimes, our demons reside in the dark recesses of the mind, and we're not conscious of their content or power. Internalized anger, pain, feelings of unworthiness, and loss of control can lead to behaviors that wreak havoc in daily life. Some of us have done things that we regret. Also, traumatic experiences from the past now remain as painful, deeply buried secrets. To escape pain and past trauma, we often develop addictive patterns to numb out and be free from constant nagging thoughts. Drugs, alcohol, smoking, binge-watching television, overeating, compulsive shopping, excessive computer and phone use, gambling, and sexual addiction can consume our lives. No wonder we cannot sit down, relax, and feel at ease in silence.

Releasing pain by becoming aware of what controls our behavior not only heals our wounds but also enables us to increase our mental and emotional health. Our bodies relax as stress wanes. We become more flexible. We change the things we can and accept the things we cannot change. In this way, we establish healthy boundaries in relationships, learn to be patient, and mitigate the need for immediate gratification. Emotions no longer overwhelm us, and we learn to *respond* to life's situations instead of *reacting* to them. We become less controlling and can engage in deep, meaningful relationships, savor time alone, and indulge in self-care. In this growing state of ease, we are in touch with our creative, spontaneous selves. We live more in the present moment where we become one with the power that moves through us, the flow of universal energy.

Life is full of wonderful and empowering moments, but research shows we tend to remember more negative thoughts and occurrences than positive ones. As we unravel our past, we reveal painful, draining emotional blocks. But we can also examine the happy, nourishing times, as these wholesome, nurturing experiences can be fertilizer for growing the capacity to inhabit the present moment fully.

Release What Weighs You Down ~ Embrace What Lights You Up Exercises and Rituals

We've all experienced emotional and physical hurt. For example, when we were young, many of us were reprimanded when we exhibited unruly emotions, and at times, our inner landscape was ignored by caregivers. As a survival mechanism, we learned to react to threats by using certain behaviors. The intention of *Roadmap to Ease* is twofold. First, it helps you recognize the heavy, detrimental baggage you've been carrying during your life's journey so you can now release it. Secondly, it helps you remember what brought you great joy and connection when growing up so you can fully open to what lights you up now.

To do this, you'll identify your core limiting beliefs, along with their accompanying resentment and hurt that have shaped your life and kept you feeling caged and reactive. You'll *feel* all this, accept it, then release it. Using the reframing techniques offered in the section, Release What Weighs You Down, below will be very helpful. For example, if you were hurt because you felt invisible to your mother, you may realize that you withdraw when you feel invisible to other people. To reframe that story, recall all the enjoyable activities you experienced with your mother and how it made you feel. This shifts your view from a limited belief to a more accurate and inclusive life story. This new insight will help you be mindful so that when you feel invisible to others in a current situation, you'll recognize why you are feeling and reacting the way you do.

Once you let go of what weighs you down, you'll focus on what lights you up. Although the tendency is to rehash painful past events, there are also happy and empowering events that shaped who you are today. You'll remember your familial relationships, best friends, adventures, beloved pets, work experiences, and mentors. Your strength and resilience today can be traced back to the love you felt, the accomplishments you were proud of, the kindness you exhibited, or the people who recognized or fostered your uniqueness.

A poignant example of this is demonstrated in a personal experience with a mentor during my high school art class, in which the teacher, Mr. Garner, acknowledged my skill and enthusiasm. After noticing that I was interested in lapidary, he shared his beautiful stone collection with me and taught me how to fashion semi-precious gems into jewelry. He mentored and encouraged me at every opportunity. Perhaps without knowing it, he taught me to trust my ability and creativity, which has continued to this day. He recognized something in me that, at the time, I didn't see in myself. When I questioned my creative ability at different points in my life, I remembered Mr. Garner's encouragement, and it inspired me to stay in the creative lane of life.

Release What Weighs You Down

You can't change traumatic or hurtful events in your past or harm you have caused, but you *can* heal from these experiences. The following mindset shifts and tools will assist you during this process.

- **Choose to let go** – The first step in letting go is to decide you're ready to leave past hurt behind and are no longer willing to rehash stories that don't serve you.

It's helpful to compose a mantra that feels empowering. When your thoughts or emotions related to past hurts surface, say the mantra to assist in the healing process. For example, "I have released that story, and I'm breathing into open-hearted forgiveness."

- **Forgive** – When you forgive, you cut the cord that tethers you to the person who hurt you. Remember, forgiveness doesn't mean that you must forget that person or how they hurt you. But when you cut the cord, you release yourself from the weight of the hurt and free up the life energy you spent rehashing and re-experiencing past hurts in the present. You will also recognize the things you want to forgive yourself for from your past.

- **Reframe** – When a life situation unfolds, you almost immediately decide its meaning and construct a story that the subconscious mind memorizes. Using a cognitive reframing technique helps you shift your mindset and view a situation, a person's behavior, or a relationship from an altogether different perspective. When your viewpoint changes, the meaning you've prescribed to the person or situation changes, which, in turn, changes your thinking and behaviors. You can't change your past, but you can reframe how you think about it and, ultimately, how you feel about it.

Getting Your Feet Wet

I designed a guidebook for participants in my course, *Following the Roadmap to Ease*, to help them practice what they learn in class. The course and guidebook are available at *www.eLayneKelley.com*.

One of the core lessons I teach is the *Deep Dive,* an exercise that guides an examination of one's past. I help you learn how to tap into the subconscious mind and gain freedom from its programmed script. I am offering an introduction to this practice with the following exercise, *Getting Your Feet Wet,* so that you can get a sense of this transformative work within a short time commitment. You can utilize it now as you move through *Roadmap to Ease.*

Let's get acquainted with it. *Getting Your Feet Wet* consists of PART ONE: Release What Weighs You Down and PART TWO: Embrace What Lights You Up, which both can be completed in an hour or two. You can do both parts on the same day or on two separate days. *Getting Your Feet Wet* opens the door to information concealed in your inner landscape and sets you on the road to liberation. From this new vantage point, you'll learn to view the world as it truly is instead of viewing it through the lens of stories you've constructed; stories that keep your thoughts in the past or future.

PART ONE helps you recognize the heavy, detrimental baggage you've carried along life's journey. In this exercise, you'll have the opportunity to bring awareness to your core limiting beliefs, resentments, traumas, and hurts that have shaped your life and kept you feeling caged. You might have different life stories than other people, but many underlying themes are similar. You may feel trapped by behaviors like being the "good girl," which is not a traumatic event but a freedom robbed, nonetheless. It's an opportunity to reflect on times when you felt shame, withdrew from friends and family, or thought you weren't enough. You may remember times when you were triggered and realize the consequences of your reactions. Ultimately, you will release all the things that no longer serve you. The chart below, *Observe and Embrace What Weighs Your Down*, lists unhealthy ego traits to help you identify qualities and behaviors that might rob your peace of mind and distance you from your soulful self.

Observe and Release What Weighs You Down

Observe When You Are...

Gossiping ◎ Worrying ◎ Complaining
Overthinking ◎ Oversharing ◎ Overindulgent ◎ Expectant
Procrastinating ◎ People Pleasing ◎ Projecting
Ungrateful ◎ Materialistic ◎ Stressed ◎ Depressed
Impatient ◎ Disengaged

Observe When You Feel...

Overwhelmed ◎ Anxious ◎ Jealous
Regretful ◎ Controlling ◎ Resentful ◎ Guilty ◎ Frustrated
Self-Doubt ◎ Unworthy ◎ Pressured ◎ Ridged
Insecure ◎ Lonely ◎ Restless ◎ Inhibited ◎ Possessive
Obsessive ◎ Pessimistic ◎ Compulsive

Observe When You Are Being...

Judgmental ◎ Perfectionistic ◎ Manipulative
Dishonest ◎ Indecisive ◎ Neglectful ◎ Argumentative
Addictive ◎ Defensive ◎ Impatient ◎ Inflexible

PART TWO inspires you to remember events and situations that made you happy and empowered or where you felt capable, curious, kind, or excited. You will also reflect on times when you felt strong, wise, brave, and connected to something larger than yourself. When did you take a risk and it worked out? Was there a skill you wanted to learn, and you had the focus and tenacity to do it? You will embrace your successes and the things that light you up! The chart below, *Observe and Embrace What Lights You Up*, lists healthy ego traits to help you identify qualities and behaviors that will enhance the quality of your life, so you feel happy and at ease.

Observe and Embrace What Lights You Up

Observe When You Are...

Focused ◎ **Kind** ◎ **Appreciative**
Honest ◎ **Easygoing** ◎ **Supportive** ◎ **Trusting** ◎ **Generous**
Humble ◎ **Laughing** ◎ **Peaceful** ◎ **Giving**

Observe When You Feel...

Inspired ◎ **Creative** ◎ **Centered** ◎ **Loving**
Calm ◎ **Happy** ◎ **Free** ◎ **Loved** ◎ **Energized**

Observe When You Are Being...

Creative ◎ **Empathetic** ◎ **Loving**
Tolerant ◎ **Brave** ◎ **Thoughtful** ◎ **Wise** ◎ **Adaptable**
Cooperative ◎ **Curious** ◎ **Gentle**
Nurturing ◎ **Playful** ◎ **Balanced** ◎ **Patient** ◎ **Attentive**

You'll know you are ready to take on *Getting Your Feet Wet* if you've been rehashing one or two painful experiences that you're ready to release or if you have a recurring story or theme that echoes in your mind. Maybe you wish the outcome was different, that you hadn't been mistreated, that your parent(s) had loved you unconditionally, or that you hadn't acted unconsciously or selfishly toward someone you loved. These are examples of the big hurts you know you're carrying and are ready to release, along with the resulting resentments, shame, or regret. Other heavy baggage you might be prepared to let go of are limiting beliefs and behaviors that stop you in your tracks, like perfectionism, feeling you're not good enough, or being stuck in the quagmire of pessimism. Other questions are listed below to help you remember as many weighty things as possible that you've been lugging around so you can acknowledge them and then release them.

A key element to both PARTS ONE and TWO is a healing ritual. Ritual *heals*.

Rumi said, "The wound is the place where the light enters you."

Our core psychological wounds and trauma are stored in the subconscious mind and in the body. These wounds show up in our everyday lives as feelings of unworthiness and anxiety, emotions out of control, and feeling disconnected from our soulful selves. By doing healing work like this, we recognize our wounds, allowing them to open so light enters.

A healing ritual invites you to pause and create a sacred experience. Ritual punctuates a holy occurrence that is forever etched in one's mind. In the future, when your mind takes you back to an unpleasant event that you've released, close your eyes and breathe deeply. Take a moment to "see" the release ceremony from your mind's eye and "feel" the release you experienced in your body. You will become anchored in healing instead of reliving hurt or carrying resentments. Take time to do this ritual whenever you're carrying weighty issues. New Year's Eve is a perfect time to leave any wounds behind and start the New Year with something that lights you up and empowers you.

PART ONE: Release What Weighs You Down Instructions

Preparation

- Choose a place where you will not be interrupted for an hour or two.
- Gather your journal and pen.

Creating the Space

- Create a calm, relaxing space – make a cup of tea and turn off your phone.
- Settle into the place you've chosen to do the exercise.

Doing the Work

- Take a deep breath in through your nose, mentally saying 'letting,' and release it slowly through your mouth, mentally saying 'go,' along with any tension in your body. Do this at least five times.

Write the following inquiry questions in your journal.

- What feelings did I suppress?
- What beliefs did I adopt because of this situation or incident?

- What behaviors did I adopt?
- What unhelpful or negative character traits did I develop, and who modeled those behaviors?
- What do I long for that I didn't receive as a child?
- What are the other messages from the past that keep me stuck today?
- What stories about specific incidents do I repeatedly tell?

- Think about your life from your first memories to the present day. Ponder each question for a few minutes, and if something pops into your mind to let go of, write your response in your journal. These questions are meant to jog your memory about repetitive themes that feel weighty, emotionally charged, and energy-draining.

- You began this exercise knowing you had one or two things you've hung onto that no longer serve you, and by pondering these questions, you might have added to that list. Now, take the stories and behaviors you want to release and turn each response into "I" statements, using phrases like, "I release, I forgive, I will." For example, your father abandoned your family when you were young. By doing this exercise, you realized two things: you've been repeating the story about your dad leaving your entire life, and you realize you never formed deep relationships with significant others for fear of being abandoned. You might write, "I release the belief that if I get emotionally close to people, they will leave me. I forgive my father for leaving the family." Write down everything you wish to release and what you want to be forgiven.

Now that you've taken the stories that have weighed you down, as well as your limiting beliefs, their resulting behavior, suppressed emotions, and resentments, and turned them into "I" statements, it's time to let it all go. When you are ready, continue with the Release What Weighs You Down Ritual that follows.

Ritual

Preparing

- Choose a safe and relaxing place for your ritual. Find a beautiful spot in nature or a comfortable place inside where you won't be interrupted.
- Gather your list, lighter, and digging tool. If you do the ritual inside, or if you do it outside and won't be digging a hole, gather a glass or stainless-steel bowl and water to fill it.
- If you have jewelry or amulets that give you comfort or align with your power, set them aside to bring to your ritual.

Creating the Space

- Once you are in the place to do your ritual, settle in.
- Quiet yourself, breathe deeply, and relax your body and mind.
- Set an intention to open your heart to forgiveness for yourself and others.

The Ritual

- Dig a small hole. If you aren't digging, fill the container you brought with water.

- Slowly read your list of statements of stories, limiting beliefs, wounds, and resentments.
- When you are ready, close your eyes and do these four things:
  - 🌸 Identify the places in your body where you feel these beliefs have been stored.
  - 🌸 Breathe into those places.
  - 🌸 Sit with any feelings that may arise, acknowledge them, and let them move through you.
  - 🌸 When the spirit moves, open your eyes.
- Light the paper. As it burns, say any of the following (most importantly, speak words that ring true for you) as ashes fall into the hole or bowl of water.

  I release you.
  I release my pain.
  I release my expectations.
  I release shame.

- Cover the hole with dirt and pour the water on top of the dirt. If you are inside, take your bowl of water and candle to the sink. As you pour the water down the sink, say the words...letting go...or words that feel meaningful.
- Breathe love into your heart, acknowledging this moment as a turning point. Sit for a few minutes and bring awareness of how light you feel after this release.
- In closing, thank yourself for taking the time to perform this healing ritual, which immersed you in peace and freedom.

When you complete the healing ritual and are ready, you can move on to PART TWO: *Embrace What Lights You Up.* You'll reflect on experiences in your life that light you up and bring you joy, ease, happiness, and a sense of freedom. You will also identify empowering qualities you possess and give them the spotlight instead of your strengths being overshadowed by limiting beliefs.

PART TWO: Embrace What Lights You Up Instructions

It's time to celebrate the buoyancy you felt after releasing painful and limiting beliefs. Now, you can fully embrace your unique qualities and strengths.

Preparing

- Choose a place to do this work where you will feel comfortable and safe.
- Carve out an hour or two, so you won't be interrupted while doing this exercise.
- Gather your journal, pen, incense, and candle.

Creating the Space

- Create a calm, relaxing space – make a cup of tea, turn off your phone, and light the incense and a candle.
- Settle into the place where you will do the exercise.

Doing the Work

- Take a deep breath in through your nose, mentally saying the word "letting," and release it slowly through your mouth, mentally saying the word "in." Feel your body relax. Do this at least five times.

Write the following inquiry questions in your journal.

- Who cheered you on when you had a win?
- What are the happy stories from your past that you retell?

- What did you look forward to doing, or what people were you excited about seeing?
- What strengths and empowering character traits did you develop, and who modeled those traits?
- What activities or people made you feel the most alive and creative?
- When did you feel free, happy, and at ease?
- What were your big Aha! Moments?

- Think about your life from your first memories to the present day. Ponder each question for a few minutes. These questions will bring memories about significant people and times you felt happy, secure, loved, and in the flow of life. You might also remember situations and interactions where you felt competent and at ease.
- Now, write in your journal all the experiences and feelings you recall about being truly happy and those that gave you a sense of freedom and creative flow. Write about the strengths and healthy character traits you recognized from your past.

Upon completing the Embrace What Lights You Up exercise, you are ready to experience the Embrace What Lights You Up ritual below.

Ritual

Preparing:

- Choose a quiet place, either inside or in nature, where you won't be interrupted.
- Gather your journal, phone, candle, incense, and lighter.
- When you did the Embrace What Lights You Up exercise, you named the qualities and strengths you've demonstrated throughout your lifetime. Now, you will use these strengths and qualities to write a list of statements to keep in your journal for this exercise and to refer to often.
- For this ritual, you will use stream-of-consciousness writing, sometimes called automatic writing. If you are unfamiliar with this type of writing, it means don't self-edit. Automatic writing bypasses the critical mind and taps into your subconscious mind, allowing insight and self-discovery. Simply write down the first words or thoughts that go through your mind without planning or consciously thinking about what you are writing. Your writing will likely flow in poem or paragraph form.

Creating Space

- Put on calming music.
- Sit comfortably. Take a few deep breaths to relax and get centered.

The Ritual

- Read over your journal entries about what made you happy during your lifetime and reflect on the quality strengths you developed. From these entries, write your statements beginning with the word "I," and then add to the phrase qualities you embody. For example, some of your qualities and strengths are tenacity, truthfulness, kindness, and curiosity. From those words, your statements might be, "I do hard things." "I speak my truth." "I follow my instincts." "I trust myself." "I have an open heart." "I am kind and curious." "I have found my voice."

- Choose the statement that feels the most empowering and freeing to you. Title a page in your journal, 'Embracing What Lights Me Up,' and write the statement you chose on the first line of the page.
- Set a timer for 15 minutes.
- Begin by using stream-of-consciousness writing described above.
- Once you have finished, read it aloud.
- Let the words sink in. If emotions surface, feel them. Breathe into them.
- Finish the ritual by reading the "I" statements aloud. Let them nurture you.
- Sit in this space until you feel centered and nurtured.

Quantum Leap

Congratulations on doing the work to clear the path to enlightenment! You are brave and can do hard things. Most of us would rather have our teeth pulled than dredge up painful memories. Excavating old hurts is uncomfortable and makes one feel vulnerable and tender-hearted. But there is great freedom when we release imprisoned feelings and disentangle ourselves from the stories of the past. Although life will continue to present challenges that can restimulate past hurts, you now have the memory of the burning ritual and what it feels like to let go. Reflect on this. Take a few deep cleansing breaths: two short breaths through your nose and one breath slowly released through your mouth. Whenever a memory of a past hurt is restimulated, take the time to do the healing ritual in the Release What Weighs You Down exercise.

In the ritual section of Embrace What Lights You Up, you created many "I" statements to use in automatic writing. Feel free to revisit the "I" statements often and pick a statement to do a stream-of-consciousness writing exercise in your journal. Giving the subconscious mind a forum to speak is invaluable in recognizing the unconscious patterns that control us.

Are you ready to make a quantum leap on the road to ease and greater awareness? In Trail Marker 4, you will meet the Watchful Observer and learn how to gain distance from your thoughts, behaviors, and actions from a detached, non-judgmental perspective. As you practice transforming your consciousness by becoming the Watchful Observer, you will recognize when you are self-critical and learn to move past self-deprecating internal messaging. From the Watchful Observer's expansive view, you'll recognize the ego's fearful and self-limiting beliefs and shift to spacious awareness. Learning to cultivate this perspective is one of our worthiest endeavors. Let's do this!

Simple Mindfulness Shifts

Simply watch your reactions to daily life situations without judgment. This will engage the Watchful Observer.

"See" your thoughts and conversations drifting by on "thought bubbles."

When you feel reactionary and are about to express a strong opinion that might be better left unsaid, ask where that strong opinion came from. Experiment with not expressing your opinion and notice if your desire to share it fades.

The Second Shift
Become the Watchful Observer

"Thoughts, when disengaged from our attention, fade into the background. Instead of having a megaphone, they are just distant whispers."

— e'Layne Kelley

The Cost of an Undisciplined Mind

Buddha observed that the mind is like a monkey that never stays still. This means the nature of the mind is anxious, complex, and restless. These hindrances produce a disturbed mind, which is just like a foolish monkey. And isn't this just how it is when thoughts swing around the mind like monkeys in a tree, helter-skelter, each competing for attention?

It's said that Buddha urged his disciples to discipline themselves to become more like a forest deer and less like a monkey swinging from tree to tree. Be like the deer that remains alert, quiets distractions, and focuses on the here and now. This discipline, this shift from monkey to deer, can bring relief and calmness to your life, a step toward a more peaceful mind.

In the undisciplined mind, the inner critic chatters loudly like the monkey. I bet you're very familiar with the inner critic's voice from personal experience and from doing the Trail Marker 3 exercise. In the previous chapter, you acknowledged the trauma experienced, and you recognized the internalized, critical voices from your childhood that took root from disapproving, hurtful, or misinterpreted remarks of parents, teachers, and caregivers. Understanding your inner critic's origin can validate your experiences and make you feel understood. You also recognized the places you shut down to protect yourself, and now, most likely, you better understand where your inner critic originated. By doing the burning ritual, you released past hurts but still realize life events will restimulate patterns, and repetitive stories might resurface.

What is the cost we pay when we fail to recognize the nature of the unstill mind? Based on my own experience, I'd say it's enormous. Living with an undisciplined mind has several consequences, and we'll focus on two here. The first is that the inner critic's mean, deafening voice is generally constant in the undisciplined mind. Second, an unruly mind will keep us lost in thoughts about the past or future as the present moment escapes unnoticed. Daily, the loud-voiced inner critic shows up uninvited, judging your thoughts and actions. For example, when you buy a pair of pants that cost more than you usually spend, feelings of guilt begin to creep in.

The inner critic pounces immediately, "Why did you spend so much money on those pants?"
"You should have waited until you lost more weight before you bought them."

"They will sit in your closet with all that other stuff that's never been worn."

It continually assures us that we can't do anything right and keeps us distracted from the present moment. As an instrument of the self-serving ego, the inner critic, with its relentless disparagement, keeps us tethered to it by always wanting our undivided attention. The inner critic also fabricates scary scenarios, and while they don't come true most of the time, the body experiences fear as if the story is true, and the fearful energy gets stored in the body.

Besides shouldering the relentless inner critic monologues, the other significant cost of the undisciplined mind is runaway thoughts. Their fuel is our hijacked attention, distracting us from being fully present with a particular experience. As a good example, when you're on a beach walk at sunset, lost in thought, the sand beneath your feet is warm and powdery, but you don't feel it. The sky's billowy white clouds are showcased on a turquoise sky pallet, but you don't see them. Seagulls furiously squawk as they fight over discarded French fries, but you don't hear them. Evidence of red tide lingers in the air, but you don't smell it.

So why do some of us not experience 'living in the moment?' It is simply because we lack the understanding of what thoughts are and what feeds them, and consequently, they have their way with us. Trauma, shame, fear, societal conditioning, and adopted beliefs can make anyone live in the past and future, and so can thinking about obligations, expectations, or future dreams. Imagine this, you're at the grocery store, lost in thought, mentally inventorying the refrigerator's contents while planning dinner. Then you remember a doctor's appointment scheduled for tomorrow morning and think about what you'll wear, making you remember that your partner must bring the kids to school because you have to go to that doctor's appointment. A woman approaches, pulling you from your rambling thoughts.

"She looks just like my friend Mary," more incessant thinking.
"It's been a year since I've been in touch with her."
"I must put that on my to-do list as soon as I get home."

Still lost in thought, you exit the store. The sun has set, but you didn't notice. The cost of being the mind's dutiful puppet? It robs you of fully experiencing portions of life because of an inability to experience living in each present moment. Think about this. How many parenting years sped by while you were lost in thought, missing those precious fleeting moments of your children's growth? Were you distracted by what needed to be accomplished next? How many times did you wish away big chunks of life?

"I can't wait to get out of school."
"I just want to have this baby."
"I wish it were time to take my vacation."

The unruly mind blocks the creative flow of the universal consciousness and stops us from experiencing what is. It keeps us energetically *doing* and not calmly *being* and simply savoring the energy of the moment and experiencing where it moves us next. Let me introduce you to an awareness that has always been with you. When you awaken to awareness, you will have the choice to distance yourself from thoughts, bringing you a sense of ease and freedom. Initially, recognizing awareness will take focus and discipline, but shifting into spaciousness is seamless once you awaken.

Become a Watchful Observer

When you learn to view your thoughts and all things transient with non-judgment and detachment, you can get distance from your thoughts and become the observer of thoughts, the Watchful Observer, the insightful one. Please welcome the Watchful Observer to accompany you on the journey to en-lightenment. I'm sure you will find the company illuminating.

You will discover how to differentiate your thoughts from the observer of thoughts. This vantage point is like sitting in cushy theater seats, watching thoughts become speech bubbles that float by on a large screen on the stage. You do not judge them as good or bad, right, or wrong; you simply observe. In this way, you experience distance between awareness of the thoughts and thoughts themselves, unlike the denseness felt when tangled up in your rogue thoughts.

The Watchful Observer resides in this spaciousness, and with-in that spaciousness, thoughts, emotions, feelings, behaviors, and the body are constantly changing. Unlike thoughts, the Watchful Observer is unchanging, constant, and always avail-able. *It is known by many names: divinity, oneness, unified field, and universal consciousness.*

Recognizing the ever-present Watchful Observer is one of the worthiest skills anyone can cultivate. With practice, a new way of being in the world emerges, and the vantage point shifts from a limiting fear-based ego view to an infinite spacious awareness. Within this new field of vision, thoughts stream by, but they no longer have the power to stir one into frenzied be-havior. Thoughts, when disengaged from our attention, fade into the background. Instead of having a megaphone, they are just distant whispers. With voices in the head no longer de-manding attention, anxiety, fear, jealousy, and confusion dissi-pate. You will also learn to distance yourself from feelings, be-liefs, and behaviors. Consequently, one experiences a sense of ease and feels freer and more satisfied. Learning to accept life as it unfolds quiets the mind, relaxes the body, and allows one to enjoy wonder in each moment.

Sustain Your Practice of the Watchful Observer

Learning to be a Watchful Observer, the awareness that has distance from all transitory experiences moving through you, is essential to gain freedom from unnecessary suffering and is the most important consciousness shift to facilitate spiritual awak-ening. To make this practice easier, remember that you're always doing one of two things: feeding the ego or feeding the soul. While knowing that the ego thrives on fear, negative thoughts, conflict, jealousy, gossip, blame, anxiety, and shame, engaging with these thoughts and feelings will never feed your soul and will only make you feel dissatisfied. That keeps you en-gaged with the ego, and the ego will win whenever you give it attention. But the awareness that hears your thoughts is your divinity. Your individuality fades as you directly experience uni-versal consciousness in this quiet, infinite spaciousness.

The process of gaining distance from your thoughts is called cognitive defusion. It requires focus to cultivate the Watchful Observer as a constant companion. Instead of being identi-fied with and attached to your thoughts, you shift your attention away from the content of your thoughts. When practicing disengagement from thoughts, realize it might not happen immediately, but with commitment and practice, you will get unstuck from fused thoughts. With practice and mindfulness, your life will profoundly change.

Watchful Observer Practice

- Find a comfortable seat and relax. Read over this practice and experience yourself doing it in your mind's eye so you can remember it when you close your eyes to do this exercise.
- Set a timer for three minutes. Close your eyes and bring your attention to the present moment.
- Breathe slowly in through your nose and release your breath slowly through your mouth.
- Imagine you are sitting in the last row of a large, empty theater, facing the stage. The stage is empty except for a big, blank screen.
- When thoughts arise, see them as thought bubbles floating by on the blank screen. Experience the thoughts as distant and separate from you and consciously feel the spaciousness of the empty theater. Breathe into the spaciousness as you see any thoughts float by on the screen.
- When you open your eyes, try to continue feeling the spaciousness you experienced in the practice and feel the detachment from your thoughts.

The Watchful Observer Practice is one of the most important exercises in this book. Knowing you are not thoughts and experiencing distance from thoughts gives you an entirely different vantage point from which to experience life. Do this exercise often and work up to five, then seven minutes. When you do this practice, don't expect the voice in your head to go away; instead, remember not to give it attention because when you don't engage thoughts, they recede. *The goal isn't to stop thinking completely; it is to avoid giving thoughts your undivided attention.* Once you become familiar with the Watchful Observer witnessing your thoughts, you will also witness emotions, feelings, beliefs, and actions. By repeatedly doing this worthy practice, your awareness will grow exponentially. Over time, you'll be able to shift seamlessly between thoughts and awareness.

Exactly What is the Watchful Observer Watching?

Pay Attention to Thoughts, Emotions, Feelings, Beliefs and Behaviors

As we become aware of the Watchful Observer, we can objectively view our thoughts, beliefs, emotions, feelings, and actions and how they are interconnected. For example, a stressful thought makes us feel anxious, and our anxiousness makes our muscles tight. Often, we think this cycle of stress, anxiety, and muscle tightness is just the way life unfolds. When we gain distance from these cycles of behaviors, rather than reacting to situations we experience, we can choose to shift into a watchful state to experience peace and presence from a detached vantage point.

Vigilantly recognize the stories you tell over and over. These are constructed from thoughts that have become your beliefs and are the building blocks of your life.

Buddha said, "What we are today comes from our thoughts of yesterday, and present thoughts build our life of tomorrow: Our life is the creation of our mind."

Remember, it's the tireless work of the ego to imprison us in a story about who hurt us, why we didn't get what was rightfully ours, or how we're victims of an unjust situation.

By examining the stories we tell ourselves and others, we can observe the beliefs we've adopted that are based on negativity and fear. For example, your parents gifted your brother more money than they gave you. You are angry at your parents and feel cheated and betrayed. Instead of stewing in negative emotions and resenting your parents, you can reframe this story so it is more empowering. You can shift from being resentful to being grateful that you received a gift from your parents. As you get curious about why they gave money unequally, you remember your brother has a large debt from when his child was born prematurely. Instead of feeding fear and emotionally shutting down because of the situation, this shift in consciousness opens your heart.

Relatively, it's better to tell an empowering story than a disempowering one, but stories remain stories, nonetheless. They are transient. By watching the stories without being attached to them, we realize they comprise fleeting thoughts, feelings, beliefs, and behaviors. The ego unravels as we become aware of everything that is 'not us.' Enlightenment is beyond any fleeting thought or belief; it is our true nature, what we are, and the absolute, unchanging nature of existence.

Our Thoughts

Our thoughts originate from what we learned growing up. They are comprised of internalized voices from authority figures, parents, teachers, churches, social media, and institutions. Thoughts we think are true become beliefs stored in our sub-conscious mind.

Some studies estimate that we think about 60,000 thoughts daily, and others say less. Of these thoughts, about 90 percent are the same thoughts from the previous day, and about 80 percent are negative. Thoughts are involuntary and occur automatically in the brain. Often, worry consumes our thoughts. The truth is that 85 percent of the things we worry about never happen. This is downright exhausting. Imagine that you are on your deathbed only to recall all the precious moments of life you frittered away with unnecessary angst. Honestly, ask yourself, "How much time have I already given over to worry?"

Michel de Montaigne said, "My life has been filled with terrible misfortune, most of which never happened."

Let's choose a life story different from Michel's. Practicing the principles and exercises in Roadmap to Ease will reduce worry and many other time-wasting energy drains.

So, let me ask you, "Are you creating your life, or is your runaway mind directing the show?"

Most people believe they are their thoughts and that all thoughts are true. Often, there is a constant dialogue going on in the mind, so when we are engaged in an actual conversation with another person, the mind is conjuring up what we will say next. Naturally, we feel impatience arise as we wait for the person to stop talking so we can speak. This dynamic does not foster an ability to be fully present in our communication with others and impedes the ability to develop healthy relationships.

Addictions to food, drugs, alcohol, tobacco, sex, gambling, devices, and shopping are commonly known. But, thinking seldom makes the list of addictions, though it's the mother of all addictions because thoughts are what drive feelings and behaviors. So then, how do we overcome the power of an addiction to thinking? And how do we break the habit of chasing compulsive thoughts? It's by doing the Watchful Observer Practice until it becomes second nature. Gaining distance from incessant chatter will profoundly affect your life. To become more aware, watch your thoughts, continually weeding the garden in your mind. Leave only what is nourishing and life-affirming.

Our Emotions

An emotional reaction is physical, immediate, temporary, and coded in human genes. Since these reactions happen in the body, they can be measured. They occur involuntarily, independent from thought, and are a reaction to an event or situation, be it real or imagined. While theorists differ on the exact number of emotions and how to classify them, the six basic emotions are:

- Fear
- Sadness
- Disgust
- Anger

- Surprise
- Joy

The body has instinctual, primal reactions to external circumstances. These emotional reactions in the body are biochemical and occur in the amygdala in the brain. Fight-or-flight is one such reaction involving the 'reptilian brain' that takes control when survival is compromised. For example, if a shark were to chase you, your body would experience a massive infusion of adrenaline to provide the fuel needed to escape, causing your heart to pound and your hands to shake. A fight-or-flight reaction is necessary when survival is at risk. Because this physiological reaction is a response to feeling threatened, a rude comment from a friend can trigger a body reaction, like the reaction to being chased by a shark. This is why the body experiences a physical reaction when we are emotionally triggered. We can also be triggered by a situation that is like a previous experience. For example, being in a serious car accident in which the last thing you remember before the crash is the sound of brakes screeching. Since that accident, when you hear screeching brakes, your body shakes, and your blood pressure spikes. Other similar traumatic events can also cause loss of sleep, depression, and mood swings.

Do the Gain Emotional Release Practice below to gain freedom from these emotional reactions. As with any persistent mental health issues, it's prudent to reach out to a therapist for help.

Gain Emotional Release Practice

🌸 **Look at what triggers you.**

Images in scary movies, certain people, places, or sounds can trigger emotions. You can also react emotionally because you feel criticized, judged, rejected, or attacked.

🌸 **Look at where the triggers originated.**

It could be from childhood or a deep-seated belief. Often, we know the specific trigger that causes us to feel threatened, but we don't know its origin. Still, we can work with a reaction to calm the reptilian brain.

🌸 **Ask yourself what you needed that you didn't get.**

In the example of the car accident, maybe you were tended to physically, but you couldn't express the fear you felt at the time, so you repressed it.

🌸 **Give yourself what you needed but did not receive at the time of the incident.**

Again, using the example of the car accident, you can ask your partner or friend to hold you while you get in touch with the fear you experienced so you can release the pent-up feelings you've been internalizing since the accident. You might decide instead to get a counselor or bodyworker to help you express repressed emotions.

Our Feelings

Feelings can teach us. Some of the feelings we can experience are love, worry, happiness, contentment, dissatisfaction, gratitude, inspiration, and annoyance. Feelings are distinct from emotions. Feelings are mental associations, and emotions are biological reactions we experience. In other words, emotions occur in the body, and feelings occur in the brain. We then experience a feeling *after* we experience a particular emotion.

Memories, beliefs, and prior experiences influence feelings themselves. They usually take place at a subconscious level and can't be measured the way that the body's reaction can. While emotions are intense and temporary, feelings are subtle and can be long-lasting. The biochemical reaction of emotion is universal, and feelings are experienced individually. When we experience a feeling, we do one of two things: spring into action or avoid the action.

Both emotions and feelings can drive behavior. When we are unaware of how emotions and feelings dictate our interactions with others, reactionary behaviors can lead to unhappiness. If we don't break the patterns of reactionary behaviors as adults, we usually exhibit the same reactions as the ones we demonstrated as a child. When we were angry as a child, we had emotional outbursts and threw things; chances are that will also be our reaction as adults.

Our Beliefs

While we can have thousands of thoughts running through the mind each day, not every thought becomes a belief. However, a repetitive thought we assume is true can become a belief. These beliefs help us to understand the world and give us a sense of safety. Once we adopt a belief, it becomes ingrained in the subconscious. We use these beliefs to judge if an event or person is good or bad, right or wrong, acceptable or unacceptable, pretty or ugly, safe or dangerous. Our beliefs also determine our decisions about what we can achieve.

As we explored in Trail Marker 3, we form core beliefs based on what we've regarded as truths received during interactions from our past with our parents, caregivers, friends, teachers, and pastors. Since most beliefs are formed during our youth, we accept as truth and without question what we have been told, being too young to discern for ourselves.

The beliefs locked in our subconscious mind are either limiting or empowering. Limiting beliefs sabotage us from becoming our best selves and from realizing our full potential. Empowering beliefs give us the confidence to attain our goals and achieve what we want out of life. Our work is to recognize our limiting beliefs because they fuel our inner critic. Our limiting beliefs become apparent as we watch our thoughts, behaviors, and the contents of our internal dialogue. Our subconscious mind will contain contents that our conscious mind remains unaware of, but we can still rewrite the subconscious. In fact, the following chapters are full of information and practices to help you do just that.

Our Behavior

Some neuroscientists estimate that about 95% of behaviors, decisions, and emotions result from programming in the subconscious mind. Behavior is an interplay between thoughts, feelings, and actions. Our actions are influenced by genetics, values, faith, norms, culture, and attitude, to name a few. We deem behaviors as acceptable or unacceptable based on what we believe. So, the importance of watching our behavior can't be overemphasized. We gain a wealth of information, casting the eye of the Watchful Observer on our actions and the behaviors we exhibit when interacting with others. For example, I might notice I am impatient every time I stand in line waiting to check out in a store. But when I recognize my impatience, I can become aware of how the stress of impatience feels in my body. Observing this simple practice can offer a wealth of information. Illuminating unconscious behavior can become a catalyst for significant behavioral change.

Here's an example of a common experience. When my partner watches the news on TV, I notice that I silently keep track of how long they've been watching. My mind also takes inventory of what they promised to do but haven't. I notice the stress my reaction is causing in my body and realize I have been silently keeping score each time they watch TV news. I may also realize that I judge them when they watch the news because I think it's a waste of time. I find myself stewing in judgment and resentment when I haven't expressed anything directly to them.

In this example, I was living in a story in my mind and not living in the present moment. With the story about my partner watching the news, I could have told them what I was thinking, which could have started a conversation that resulted in both of us learning and growing. Remember, you have many choices of how to handle situations when observing repeated behaviors that cause stress. You could change your reaction from judging your partner and stop taking an inventory of what your partner isn't doing and instead focus on all the things they do that are worthy of appreciation.

Sometimes, though, you might realize that what you are doing indicates deep-seated issues with your partner. When this is the case, you can choose to talk to a therapist. In either case, you shift your focus toward something you can change in yourself rather than attempting to change a partner. And, of course, you can also continue the behavior and make no change at all. The beauty is that when you engage the Watchful Observer and feel the weight of reliving the same behaviors, you are inclined to start making choices that give rise to feeling lighter and happier.

"Does this behavior make me feel heavy and dense, or does it make me feel light and expansive?" is a helpful question to ask yourself. Another good question might be, "Why haven't I expressed my feelings to my partner?"

Ways to Cultivate Self-Awareness

Self-awareness is simply having the clarity to monitor your inner world. You understand your thoughts, feelings, and actions and realize why you do what you do. In general, self-aware people are happier and find deeper meaning in life. Thoughts do not control them, and they don't experience emotional outbursts because they have learned how to self-regulate. They listen to others mindfully and cope with another's emotions calmly. They attempt not to take things personally. Change, conflict, or new concepts are generally not experienced as a threat. Victim consciousness is diminished because they've learned to take responsibility for their actions, and egocentric needs no longer control them. Having healed their inner wounds, kindness and empathy radiate from genuinely self-aware people.

1. Develop Emotional Intelligence

Emotional intelligence is the ability to understand what causes an emotional response in us and to be aware of each particular response as it occurs. We can then access this awareness and observe specific actions as we navigate relationships.

One necessary element to develop emotional intelligence is self-awareness. There are two types of self-awareness – internal and external. Internal self-awareness is having insight into one's personality and being conscious of strengths and weaknesses, thoughts, emotions, beliefs, and motivations. With practice, we become aware of what we do and why. External self-awareness is the ability to understand how people perceive us as they observe how we communicate and behave, simply put, the impact our words and actions have on others. Being aware of how our words and actions are received by others is key to effective communication and deeper connection. To understand how they perceive us we can ask for feedback, observe how people respond in our interactions, ask open-ended questions, and observe body language. Ranking high on one type of awareness doesn't mean we are also adept in the other.

Emotional and behavioral responses are established in early childhood, usually from ages two to five, and become the unconscious assumptions and beliefs that will dictate 95 percent of adult behavior. For instance, "There is never enough money."

"I am not worthy of love."
"Everybody leaves me."
"People can't be trusted."

Have you had an experience in which someone says something to you, and your heart begins to race immediately, and your palms sweat? This emotional reaction feels like a fight-or-flight response and occurs because whatever is said touches upon our subconscious assumptions and beliefs.

These subconscious assumptions and beliefs riddle the body with undue stress elicited by fear, anger, envy, jealousy, anxiousness, hopelessness, and greed, to name a few. Unless this cycle is broken, we are destined to ride a rollercoaster of emotions that results in a toxic body and mind and creates a general state of exhaustion and unhappiness.

2. Access Clues Found in the Past

In Trail Marker 3's Release Your Pain – Embrace Your Power exercise, you likely gained valuable information about your triggers. While the exercise explored the past and released flawed beliefs and resentments, daily events can and most likely will still trigger you. The more you remain conscious of what triggers your reactions, the easier it will be to engage the Watchful Observer and to respond to current life situations rather than react the way you may have in the past.

3. Engage in Meditation and Practice Mindfulness

The more one practices mindfulness and meditation, the sooner the ability to shift to a Watchful Observer consciousness will become second nature. Insight Timer is my go-to app for thousands of meditations and a wonderful place to connect to a global community. As its name says, it's a timer and tracks your daily progress. You can also access the Watchful Observer Meditation I've recorded by going to *www.eLayneKelley.com/theWatchfulObserver*.

4. Recognize Others as a Mirror of Yourself

Stoic philosopher Marcus Aurelius posed this question, "What fault of mine most nearly resembles the one I am about to criticize?"

When someone else's behavior annoys or disturbs us, we may find upon closer examination that we behave the same way, yet don't recognize this. Moreover, it is generally a behavior that we have an aversion to, so in essence, we judge the 'other' instead of judging ourselves – often because we are not yet aware that we possess the behavior. So, when you find yourself aggravated by what someone says or does, pause and take an honest inventory of yourself, reflecting on which traits and behaviors they demonstrate, which you might exhibit as well.

5. Express Yourself on Paper

Devote one journal specifically for entries about your experiences when you engage the Watchful Observer. When you practice watching your thoughts, beliefs, feelings, and behaviors, jot down any aha moments as they occur. Take five minutes at the end of each day to write specific examples of your realizations. At the end of the week, read the daily entries. This practice helps you recognize renegade thoughts and patterns in your behaviors and reveals life's transitory nature.

6. Adopt an Attitude of Openness

To explore what makes us tick requires vulnerability. And so, we tend to shy away from uncomfortable emotions, finding it easier to avoid looking at our perceived weaknesses. But then, having an attitude of curiosity, willingness, and bravery when engaging the Watchful Observer is extremely helpful. Do not label emotions, feelings, or reactions to circumstances as 'good' or 'bad.' When you practice, you are just watching. Be compassionate and non-judgmental and strive to interject levity. Be willing to take responsibility for your triggers. Remember, you are simply gathering information to identify reactions and patterns that no longer serve your well-being.

7. Seek Healthy Feedback

Why is it helpful to seek feedback, and what kind of issues might we want feedback about?

Because we are often raised with criticism, not constructive feedback, we may feel vulnerable when we request it. Also, just the idea of asking for feedback may seem counterintuitive. To mitigate some of these concerns, ask for feedback from someone you trust, such as a longtime friend or spouse. A parent may or may not be a good choice depending on your relationship, power dynamics, and the possibility of triggers arising based on your history with them.

Begin with a minor, specific issue. This enables the person giving feedback to experience how you react to their reflection and you to theirs. Be aware if you are feeling defensive. You might feel tender but breathe and attempt to remain neutral when listening to their feedback. When they finish their feedback, thank them for sharing their perspective. There is no need to discuss what they have told you, so don't argue their point of view or defend your position. Process what they've shared in your own time and glean wisdom from feedback that may be helpful, letting go of anything that doesn't ring true.

Your constant companion, the Watchful Observer, accompanies you as you continue the journey toward enlightenment, along with skills you've learned here to cultivate self-awareness and greater access to universal consciousness. The next stop, Trail Marker 5, addresses the third shift, teaching how to live in the NOW. Please take a deep breath into your belly, release it slowly through your mouth, and turn the page.

I'll meet you at the trailhead.

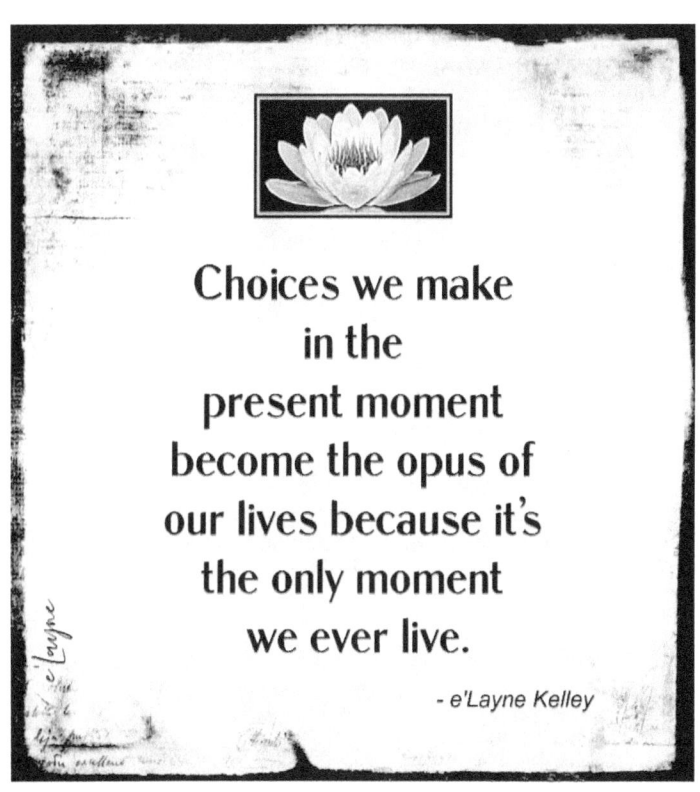

Choices we make
in the
present moment
become the opus of
our lives because it's
the only moment
we ever live.

- e'Layne Kelley

Simple Mindfulness Shifts

To practice accepting 'what is' when a life situation makes you feel reactionary, simply stop and breathe until the feeling passes.

If you haven't already, introduce meditation into your daily routine. It is the most important practice on the path to ease, freedom, and happiness. Start with a short period of time and add more time when you're ready.

If possible, go into nature for a few minutes every day. Feel the air on your skin and the sun on your face. Listen to the sounds and breathe in the smells.

The Third Shift
Living in the NOW

*"There was a moment before this moment. It will not come
again."*

– e'Layne Kelley

What it Means to Live in the NOW

Many layers of awakening will be revealed to you along the
path to enlightenment. The encouraging news is that you can
take simple steps as your infinite self is revealed. Ultimately, life
is forever changed once the veil between the ego and divinity
is lifted. No longer are you ruled by material longings, voices in
the mind, addictive habits, reactive emotions, or rote behaviors. Instead, you will experience immense freedom of a calm
mind and be filled with gratitude, awe, love, and ease.

The soul's journey toward divine consciousness is the most piv-
otal work in anyone's lifetime. So, what veils ever-present divinity from your awareness? What keeps you from co-creating
with source energy a deeply satisfying life? More than likely,
your attention is laser-focused on constant thoughts in your

head that block creative source energy, preventing it from moving through you. If any of these voices inside your head were another person, would you want to hang out with them? Would you enjoy having a conversation? Would you find them engaging? Annoying?

Living in the present doesn't mean excluding past or future thoughts since they are necessary to conduct daily life. For example, if you intend to meet a friend at a concert, you must buy advance tickets and plan a meeting time. Day-to-day activities like attending school, getting a job, and raising a family take planning. The thoughts it takes to make life run smoothly aren't the thoughts that trip us up. We want to watchfully observe thoughts and discern the ones that hijack our attention. To decern, we choose to focus our awareness on the quality of thoughts, how they make us feel, and the degree of attachment we have to them.

When we think about the past, we want to be aware of when we're tangled in a mind loop of regret and blame and repeatedly rehashing the same stories with no positive change. Looping back to negative thoughts continually wires subconscious beliefs, creating patterns that erode well-being. The stories we tell about our past contain a treasure trove of information about the motivations behind our actions.

Revisiting the past, as we did in Trail Marker 3, helps us recognize what needs to be weeded out, allowing space for creative energy to flow. Similarly, when we think about the future, we can get lost in fearful thoughts and wallow in unpleasant, stressful, and unproductive stories about things that may never happen. Being in the NOW is to inhabit the present experience fully. The more time you live in the NOW, the fainter the voice in your head becomes because your attention is present and not focused on thoughts. With time, the monologue in the head may become a respectful friend rather than an annoying foe.

Think about it this way: Life happens in the present moment, but when we focus only on the destination and not the journey, we can easily miss out on what life offers. The simplest way to get out of our thoughts and into the NOW is to focus on our breath.

Let's practice...

Breathe deeply in through your nose.
Feel your lungs expand.
Exhale through your mouth and feel your body relax.
Savor the present moment.

As we focus on our thoughts and how we react and respond to them, we become acutely aware that our present actions spring from beliefs, opinions, and habitual behavior from the past. Our past stories dictate current behaviors. For example, we want to run a marathon and realize the hidden reason for this desire is that we were humiliated in third grade when we lost a race. Subconsciously, we are trying to heal a childhood hurt by winning a race as an adult. Or if we grew up in a family without enough money, it may motivate us to earn $1 million as adults. Walking into the NOW is to enter a receptive mode where actions spring from the divine flow of creative energy in each present moment, not from what we think we 'should' do. We maintain goals, yes, but we know happiness doesn't rely solely on achieving goals. It's helpful to check into our current behaviors and ask, "Are these motivations in alignment with a soulful desire, or am I trying to heal a hurt from the past?"

The experience of being in the present moment is quite distinct from the experience of being caught up in the mind's dialogue. Here are two scenarios where I simply walk from my sixth-floor condominium to my car. One demonstrates being lost in thought, and the other demonstrates inhabiting the NOW.

One:

As I descend the staircase, my thoughts go like this: "How can it be so hot? It's winter. I should have worn a tank top. Got to get gas. Go to Publix. I wish I had worn my other shoes. My feet are hot. I forgot the recycling. Ice coffee? Yes, Starbucks. Hope my sunglasses are in the car."

I'm sure you know this kind of dialogue. It's similar to what you've been listening to inside your head for your entire life.

Two:

As I exit my apartment, I feel my wrist turning the doorknob. I hear the door creak as I open it. Stepping outside, I feel the sun's warmth hit my face. I open the stairwell door and start my descent down the stairs. I hear the door bang shut behind me. I feel my hand clutch the railing and hear my ring clang on the metal. I feel the railing's cool metal on my fingertips. I feel the oppressive heat in the stairwell envelop me. I see a lizard chase a bug. I hear my flip-flops slap my feet with every step.

The work is to put your attention on the task at hand, bringing you into the NOW. You are forming a habit of becoming the

Watchful Observer, so you are aware of when you're present and when you are lost in thought.

What to Take on Your Journey into Enlightenment

The path to greater awareness begins exactly wherever you are in life. Even though you addressed past hurts in Trail Marker 3, each of us embarks on this journey with things packed long ago – a suitcase stuffed with emotional baggage, a tote jammed with judgments, and a voice in the brain that never stops talking. We also bring a lifetime of stories to our adventure, along with joys, fears, and perceived limitations. Most of us won't even remember packing many beliefs and habits hauled around for years, like self-sabotage, perfectionism, criticism, and complaints. While the baggage may have clung to us uninvited, a few things to mindfully pack will serve us brilliantly on this spiritual trek: a patient attitude, an adventurous spirit, a sense of humor, a willingness to surrender ego – and an awareness of our mortality.

Walking with Death on Your Shoulder

The ego is driven to survive. Because the ego is rooted in the material world, death threatens the ego. And death is often feared in Western culture. We like certainty, and nothing is more uncertain than when death will knock on the door. We fear pain, losing loved ones, and, most of all, we fear the unknown. Yet the fear of death and a desire to keep death in the shadows can hold us back from experiencing our divinity. Whenever we deny death or disengage from the natural cycles of life, we block vital energy in the body and fuel the ego. But when we can befriend death, we accept life on life's terms, and it frees the energy spent holding back the inevitable.

I was introduced to the concept of mortality at a very young age. The first stories I remember were about death and loss. My father died when I was one month old, and so I was raised by my mother, a 27-year-old widow drowning in her disbelief and sorrow. Luckily, we moved in with my grandparents, who wrapped me in a cocoon of love. Then, at age 13, my beloved Nana also died. My heart was broken because I didn't have the chance to say goodbye to her. Many years later, my step-dad died. His death was so different because I was able to be with him. He wanted to die at home, so we enlisted hospice to help our family navigate the journey. My brother and I tended to dad's needs, comforting him as best we could. Just as someone midwifes birth, I found myself immersed in midwifing death. Death was no longer lurking in the shadows.

Witnessing death pulled back the veil between the worlds and brought the natural end of a human journey into the light. As my dad passed, I envisioned his eternal spirit soaring, living on, simply out of sight. Time spent in the present moment with those dying helps remove fear and creates an atmosphere that invites a more authentic transition.

As meaningful as these experiences are, I would have to say that my biggest lesson about mortality came from having a life-threatening disease for over four decades, undiagnosed for two. When I was finally diagnosed with hepatitis C, I had no idea whether my death was imminent or not since the disease had been replicating undetected.

Terrified, I consulted an herbalist and wise woman, who said, "It sounds like your body has made friends with the virus."

I knew then that I needed to make friends with the virus...and with death. Otherwise, I would spend the rest of my life consumed by fear.

My instincts told me to forgo risky treatment options and to nourish my body instead. I visualized death as a crow perched on my shoulder, and that crow walked with me for over two decades until a revolutionary drug came on the market, promising a cure for the disease. Although I was grateful for the opportunity to become disease-free, I was emotional about saying goodbye to the virus. Before I took the medication, I did a ritual to thank the virus for being an amazing teacher, showing me never to take a single precious day for granted. Living with the awareness that my life could end at any moment (true for all of us!), I took more chances, savored more moments, tended to my health, was a little braver, and became kinder to myself and others.

While traveling the path to enlightenment, one always walks with death on one's shoulder. Awareness of our mortality and knowing that death can come at any time helps us measure the quality of our present life.

We ask these questions often, "How would I want to spend my time if this were my last day on Earth?

- "Who do I want to be with?"
- "What feeds my soul?"
- "Is there anything left unsaid?"
- "Do I have regrets I want to address?"

We mindfully remember our mortality and stay aware that our time here is limited.

Shedding Ego, Realizing Divinity

If you were raised to value attaining external 'things' to feel successful, you might have realized that as soon as you achieved a worldly goal, there was a tendency to want yet another item or undertake another pursuit. But, when one is spiritually depleted, no amount of money, stuff, or achievements can buy them happiness. Landing a better job or becoming debt-free is fantastic but doesn't always bring inner peace. It's OK to want material belongings, take extravagant vacations, or work for the letters 'Ph.D.' after your name. However, desire can pose challenges when one's sense of self-worth hinges on material possessions, a status attained through a career, or marrying for wealth.

So, how do we attain an authentic life filled with happiness and peace? I believe it is taking the inner path to enlightenment that leads to the recognition of our true identity. **We're divine beings having human experiences**. As we come to know the nature of our being, we experience peace and happiness intrinsically.

As our minds quiet from practicing the shifts below, we find ourselves being less self-absorbed. As we become more expansive and less controlled by thoughts, addictive behaviors begin to subside. Impulses to numb out, stuff feelings with food, or judge ourselves and others also start to wane. We become aware of the distractions and restlessness that consume much of daily life – the voices inside our heads, watching television, listening to music, and using a computer or phone. Because we learn to observe these activities instead of engaging in them robotically, we begin to experience the weight we've carried from living amped-up lives. The ego kicks and screams in protest when we give up distractions, but eventually ego dims under mindfulness's spotlight.

As you internalize the practices below, you'll begin to breathe deeper without feeling rushed or restless. You'll be less reactive and more relaxed, experiencing a greater sense of well-being. The present moment will no longer slip away unnoticed. You'll spend more extended periods experiencing and savoring the NOW.

Guideposts Along the Path to NOW

Practicing simple shifts in consciousness enables us to recognize that which is ever-changing, thoughts, feelings, and behaviors, and recognize awareness, that which is constant and conscious of all that is transitory. When you shift focus away from the density of thoughts, feelings, and behaviors, you experience life in the present moment. The reactionary ego recedes as you become more aware of the source energy infinitely flowing around and through you. Your mind may not be completely quiet, but you are not totally absorbed in internal dialogue. In the light of divine consciousness, thoughts become more transparent and recessed, even distant.

Become Still – Meditation

The modern world rewards doers, achievers, movers, and shakers. The flip side of doing is being, but there aren't many awards handed out for just being. As a child, if I sat down for more than a few minutes, my mother would say, "If you don't have anything to do, I'll give you something to do." Sitting down to relax now, I still feel the impulse to busy myself. The impulse to move when we want to relax can cause restlessness and anxiety. As you train your mind to relax, your body will follow.

You can explore stillness through meditation. Set a timer for as little as ten minutes daily to sit, close your eyes, and get in touch with your breath. When you withdraw from daily distractions, meditation creates a pause to tune into your inner process. With time, you'll gain distance from your thoughts and feelings and will realize they are transitory. The Watchful Observer, that which is aware of your thoughts and feelings, will make itself known. Awareness, unlike thoughts, is constant. There is no right or wrong way to meditate in this receptive mode. Thoughts simply come and go; some grab your attention, and some float by. Your nose may itch, and your toes may cramp as you experience the sensations in your body. Breathe into feelings that surface: peace, resistance, hunger, and boredom. If you find yourself lost in thought, return your attention to the breath.

Meditation helps you distance yourself from constant thoughts and from the impulse to do. You begin to experience space between your thoughts, and in this still, quiet mind, the voice of intuition can be heard. Peaceful relaxation gained from meditation begins to transfer to your daily activities. You become more receptive, observant, and less reactionary.

Mindful of the Task at Hand

Mindfulness is a cognitive skill that brings full attention to any task at hand in the present moment. For example, when you drink tea, your hand feels the warm cup, your nose sniffs the tea's fragrance, and your ears hear the spoon clang as you stir in the honey. When you are mindful, you experience life through your senses – touch, smell, sight, hearing, and taste. When your attention is present, you directly experience what you are doing rather than being lost in the mind's conversation.

You can effortlessly practice mindfulness while doing countless daily activities. When preparing food, hear the knife hit the cutting board, feel the tears flow as onion vapors burn your eyes, and see the bright colors of the vegetables beneath your fingertips. Instead of rushing through activities, slow down and bring mindfulness to the task of washing your hair, brushing your teeth, or going on an evening walk. Let all senses awaken and become fully engaged. Other ways to practice mindfulness are by meditating, either walking, sitting, or lying down. You can also mindfully follow your breath, be mindful of your movements, feel body sensations, and bring mindfulness to eating. Remember, focused attention on the task leads you into the NOW.

Here is an insightful Zen story about living in the NOW called *Two Monks and a Woman*: A senior and a junior monk were walking down a path and came upon a river with a strong current. As they were about to cross, a woman approached and asked if they would help her cross the river. The monks looked at each other, knowing they had vowed not to touch a woman. Then, the older monk picked the woman up and carried her across the river. The monks continued their silent walk. For hours, the junior monk wanted to break the silence and question the senior monk about his actions.

Finally, he blurted out, "We are not allowed to touch a woman. How, then, could you carry that woman across the water?"

The senior monk replied, "I put her down on the other side of the river. Why are you still carrying her?"

This story is a profound example of how we can live mindfully in the present moment or live in the disturbed mind.

Back to Your Breath

Why is returning to the breath one of the easiest ways to experience the NOW? Because breath takes place in the present. We are present when we pay attention to where breath is in the body. But in truth, we take breathing for granted most of the time, and often, we only notice it when we are out of breath. Once normal breathing returns, it's out of mind once again.

Breath is a lifetime companion and fellow traveler on the enlightenment journey. Whenever we use mindfulness practices, breathing is elevated to the prominent position it deserves. Mindful breathing offers many benefits, including improved organ health, release of toxins, pain relief, digestive aid, improved posture, muscle relaxation, and more energy. When we experience fear or anger, deep breathing can quiet runaway thoughts and emotions, release tension, and provide mental clarity. Mindful breathing shifts attention away from constant thoughts, helps us get in touch with the body, and brings us into the NOW. It's an excellent antidote for anxiety because deep breathing and stress do not co-exist.

It is helpful to design a breathing practice associated with one or two tasks you do each day such as brushing your teeth, waiting for water in a kettle to boil, sitting at a red light, or standing in line at a grocery store. Anchoring mindful breathing with a specific task will remind you to enter the NOW. As you do these activities, be aware of air coming into your nose, feel your lungs filling with air and entering your belly, and experience warm air exiting through your nose. Don't change the pace of your breathing...observe your breathing. This simple practice welcomes you to the moment.

Here is another breathing technique that will quickly calm you in which you release carbon dioxide and breathe in oxygen.

- Breathe twice through the nose, feeling your breath fill your lungs and then your belly.
- Follow with an extended exhale through the mouth.
- Repeat until you feel calm.

Density Within Consciousness

When I was about 11 years old, sleep began to evade me. I attended Catholic school at that time, and the concept of burning eternally in hell deeply disturbed me. My unrelenting thoughts about mortality felt as thick as oil slug trapped in the confines of the space between my ears. I would lie in bed contemplating infinity. My vivid imagination painted terrifying pictures of humans suffering in eternal flames. My concept of a loving God didn't square with a God banishing sinners to hell for eternity.

To escape fear during restless nights, I would repeatedly experience a consciousness beyond the density of those disturbing thoughts and images. When I did, it was as though I could see my thoughts through binoculars. When the binoculars were focused on dense thoughts, nothing else had my attention except the thoughts in my head. My breathing was shallow; I felt anxious and alone. But when I widened the focus and panned out from my thoughts, the boundaries of my body began to melt. The thoughts became distant as I rested in the experience of infinity. I was no longer my thoughts, no longer my body.

Ultimately, because of these experiences, sleepless nights became time used for welcomed soul travel. I didn't realize what was happening inside me, but I was happy to gain freedom from my fear of hell's fury. I experienced the spaciousness as comforting and holy, stirring reverence and awe.

As my teenage years approached, my thinking once again ruled my life. Dense thoughts dominated my mind, but this time, they were personal storylines. I didn't feel good enough, worthy enough, pretty enough, or thin enough. My experience with infinity receded but, thankfully, returned during my early twenties, when I began a spiritual quest.

I understand now that when we focus on dense thoughts from the limited mind's vantage point, we aren't in touch with our eternal nature. Freedom, happiness, and ease await us when we shift away from unceasing and disturbing thoughts. As we develop spiritual awareness, we can explore space within and without. Inner space is found in the pause between thoughts, the pause between breaths, and the pause between an event and a reaction. When we view life from a spacious vantage point, we recognize the triviality with which we've approached much of our lives.

Ego is a dense structure that thrives on drama. But ego loses its power when we shift our consciousness from density to infinity. We are no longer attached to the declarative statements from the ego that define our identity – the vantage point shifts from being the center of the universe to being at one with the universe.

On the path toward enlightenment, you bring awareness to the dense structures in your life and infuse them with space. For example, when you are angry at a friend, your mind creates multiple stories about why they are wrong and why you are right. If you take a deep breath and observe your run-on story, you'll notice a pause in your thoughts. Let that pause expand. Go outside. Feel the space around and within you. When thoughts arise, let them drift by. This is what I did with my thoughts about burning in hell. I shifted my awareness from the dense thoughts in my head, and eventually, the thoughts floated freely in endless space. Play with the concept of density and infinity. Identify each vantage point. You will find that from an infinite, expansive view, details of the dense life where you dwell most of the time begin to lose prominence.

Accepting What Is

Life is a series of events – a raw egg slips from your hand, a car cuts you off in traffic, a child spills milk on your new outfit. Anger and frustration are often the primary emotions elicited by situations like these. But you can't return the egg to its shell, make strangers better drivers, or put spilled milk back into the cup. No matter the reaction to dropping a raw egg on the floor, it must still be cleaned up. You can rage against what you can't control, or you can *accept what is*. Once the egg splats on the floor, you can *choose* how to react. You can choose to BREATHE...create space...and not resort to the inner dialogue that spurs an emotional reaction. Remember, thoughts and feelings are on opposite sides of the same coin. Our thoughts elicit a feeling. First, we must recognize when unproductive thoughts are sweeping us away and decide we don't want to remain reactive. With this awareness, we can change our thoughts or watch our thoughts without attachment. Doing this will change how we feel and, subsequently, how we react.

When your reaction to a situation or event is an eruptive outburst, the egoic identity is in charge. Eruptive outbursts create unnecessary suffering. Yes, we want to be deeply feeling beings and don't want to repress emotions. But do we want to spend precious life energy exhausting ourselves on needless rants when we can't change the outcome? Wrestling with 'what is' can drain adrenal glands, erode self-esteem, and keep us from happiness and inner peace. Many of us don't spend our energy wisely. Reactionary patterns die hard, and it is solitary work to bring awareness to the inner landscapes of the mind, clear out the garbage of destructive thinking and volatile emotions, and reveal the infinite glow of the soul's light.

We have a choice in every moment – accept events we can't control or wage war against what is. Once you can create a space between an event and your reaction to it, you can choose to de-escalate and have time to evaluate how you want to respond. Your ability to develop this practice helps immensely in accepting life of life's terms. Embodying this practice alleviates unnecessary suffering and is a quantum leap toward happiness, ease, and freedom.

Feel Energy in Your Inner Body

Another way to get out of the mind is to experience energy moving in your inner body. When you experience your inner body, you are not listening to the voices in your head. You are in the present moment. Let me show you how.

Take a moment and sit in a comfortable position...become fully aware of your breath. This simple action immediately brings you into your inner body as you feel your breath enter the nose, feel your lungs rise on an inhale and sense your belly rise and fall with each inhale and exhale.

Now, with your eyes closed, shift your awareness to different parts of your body, starting with your hands. Focus your attention on your fingers and feel the sensations and energy moving through them. Do this for about a minute. Feel the life energy and sensations in your right foot. Does it feel warm or cool? Light or heavy? Lethargic or lively? Repeat this exercise with every part of your body.

After you've experienced the energy and sensations in parts of your body, bask in the energy of your entire body. If you lose your concentration, remember to return to your breath. Rest in inner body awareness for as long as it feels comfortable.

You can practice connecting with your inner body throughout the day. Experiment with doing it as you perform household tasks, talk with people, or walk in nature.

Go into Nature

Urban life can make us feel alone and separate from our infinite, divine self. The concrete, the rush, the noise, and the commercial distractions bring our attention outward. Communing with nature ignites feelings of magic and wonder; as time melts away, we become aware of spiritual connectivity. When in the wild, we feel smaller, less self-important, and not so in control. The ego fades in the light of all-consuming, breathtaking landscapes.

When venturing into nature with friends, we can tend to talk or overlook the subtleties of Mother Nature's gifts. To fully commune with nature, wander alone until you are drawn to an inviting place to sit. Become aware of your breath, listen to the sounds of nature cut through the quiet, feel your butt against a rock, and experience the sun warming your face and the wind blowing through your hair. Melt into your surroundings. The ego dissolves as your consciousness reaches into the vast space enveloping you. The mind quiets, stress dissipates, and euphoria enters your being. Use your powers of observation to witness the ever-changing patterns of clouds, smell the sweet perfume of gardenias, and hear huge waves pound eternally upon the shore. Feel the power of mountains that have risen majestically from the sea. Watch the animal kingdom interact seamlessly with their environment. Be at one with the present moment.

Enter the Silence

You can enter silence by practicing the exercises above that walk us into NOW. You can also enter silence by simply creating a pause. When you close your eyes and let time pass, you will experience a space between your thoughts in which to enter silence. Breathe in and let penetrating silence fill you. To exit a loud and demanding life and enter silence takes practice. Yet, devoting just ten minutes for silence upon waking or before sleep guarantees a rendezvous with divinity.

Attending a silent retreat is also a place to experience deep silence. This type of retreat may offer spiritual lectures, but you don't engage in conversation the rest of the time. If you want to be completely alone with your mind, many retreat centers rent cabins and provide meals delivered to the cabin. In either setting, being submerged in silence without using electronic devices for an extended period may surface issues that daily life distractions have buried.

Time to Get Curious

When you recognize that you are being opinionated or making assumptions about someone, you can get curious about *why* you've made assumptions rather than passing judgment on them. Are you ready to learn how to grow in awareness by asking good questions that help you gain wisdom and be less reactive, more relaxed, and more communicative? Awesome!

Then, turn the page...

Simple Mindfulness Shifts

When a challenging event arises with a friend or loved one, are you comfortable talking to them about your thoughts and feelings? Get curious about your reaction.

When you are in conversations, simply observe…later ask yourself questions like, "Did I monopolize the conversation?" "Was I really listening?" "Did I understand everything that was said?" "Could I have asked clarifying questions?"

During your daily activities, ask yourself, "How can I be more curious?" "What questions might elicit greater insight?"

The Fourth Shift
Bravely Ask Good Questions

"The wise man doesn't give the right answers, he poses the right questions."

– Levi Strauss

Get Curious

Each of us experiences our life through the lens of the ego, a persona we believe to be the 'self' or 'i.' The ego is a dynamic part of a personality that helps form beliefs about 'self' during childhood.

Each individual's viewpoint is influenced by their upbringing and many other sociological and psychological factors. Even though we have unique life experiences with differing beliefs and viewpoints, it is common to assume that other people see life through the same lens as we do. This is because most people identify with their constructed ego and don't question whether their beliefs are valid. Often, these limiting beliefs and judgments create a narrow perspective from which to view life. Still, asking yourself and others good questions can take you beyond limited beliefs, expand your consciousness, and enable you to gain new and fresh perspectives. Good questions are open-ended and solicit thoughtful, insightful answers. These questions begin with "who," "what," "when," "where," "why," and "how."

Some of us were born into environments where, as children, we learned communication skills and developed emotional intelligence. Parents modeled empathy, so we learned to be empathetic. They listened and asked good questions, which gave us a better chance of maintaining innate curiosity and becoming proactive listeners. A proactive listener intends to listen to the person talking and is mindful to attempt to understand them. Some of us could freely explore our environment during childhood, which fostered curiosity. Others weren't allowed. When innate curiosity, communication skills, and emotional intelligence aren't fostered early in life, developing these skills later can be more challenging. But anytime we learn to ask good questions, growth is always possible.

I had an experience during my first year of college that was an example of asking a good question that gave me insight into how little I knew about my emotional landscape. The psychology professor had about 20 students sit in a circle and asked us to introduce ourselves and say a few sentences about how we felt. After their introduction, each student began their sentence with, "I think..." And each time, he immediately cut them off. After everyone had their turn, we all sat in silence.

Next, he invited us to speak up when we could answer his question, "How are you presently feeling?" We all sat in silence until class ended, then walked out, some of us shaking our heads, as not one of us could articulate how we were feeling. This class experience woke me up to how out-of-touch I was with my feelings. This deficit got me extremely curious to know what made me and other people tick!

Communicating Clearly

While you walk the path to greater awareness, you can watch for mental narratives that have caused you to alienate or dismiss people. Assumptions keep you from understanding where people come from when communicating with them. As I said earlier, we often assume others think the same as we do. And when you realize they don't, it can lead to disagreements, judgments, and isolation, with all involved not feeling heard or understood. It's difficult to experience oneness when trapped in this fixed way of seeing yourself and others.

There are other reasons to misunderstand people as well. For one, while someone else is speaking, there is a tendency to get lost in one's thoughts or try to remember what your response will be when it's your turn to speak. When you do this, you aren't being present or paying attention. Also, you might judge someone's tone of voice and assume you know what it means. When you make this assumption, you might hear someone's tone and think it sounds stern when, in fact, they are simply being concise. Reading body language is another cue you may use to make assumptions based on the meaning that you perceive.

So, how do you bridge the gap you create when you project mental biases onto another? By attempting to enter conversations without assumptions and not taking a defensive posture.

When one's intention is to begin a conversation non-judgmentally, others are more likely to feel safe when communicating deeply. Also, enter conversations fully intending to pay attention to what the person is saying. Being open-minded, interested, and sincere helps create an atmosphere of openheartedness without trying to be right or getting others to buy into your belief system. Choosing to incorporate these shifts creates fertile ground for truthful communication.

Becoming a Good Listener

Feeling understood is a most important basic human need. When one doesn't feel understood, they don't feel connected to humanity. We want to know that others 'get us' because it affirms our identity and makes us feel accepted, empowered, and valued. When we don't, we can feel isolated and alone and are more prone to depression. Because of this shared need to be understood, asking good questions and becoming a good listener are essential skills to develop in order to cultivate deep relationships.

How do you become a good listener? You can ask good questions all day long but never communicate effectively if the answers to your good questions aren't heard. Quieting your mind and bringing attention to the present moment is essential for improving your listening ability. Another trait of a good listener is to hold the intention to understand what the person you are listening to is saying. To fulfill this intention, you need to disengage from distractions, turn off the TV and phone, and bring all of yourself to the conversation. Also, remain relaxed, breathe deeply, and speak in a calm voice. Be respectful and kind, speak from the heart, and bring a positive attitude. Leave opinions and the inner critic at the doorstep. And do not interrupt.

It's equally important to pay attention to your threshold for the amount of undivided attention you can give. When a conversation is completely one-sided, it's OK to stop participating. You must be an authentic listener, not just someone enduring a one-sided conversation. When you don't understand what someone is saying, ask clarifying questions. If you find your attention waning during a meaningful conversation, ask to table the discussion for another time and make a date to pick up where you left off.

Becoming a Better Communicator

Communication is a way you can feel connected to family and friends. The basis of deep friendship is intimacy. Intimacy, sometimes referred to as 'into me see,' happens when each person in a relationship lets their guard down to reveal their secrets and vulnerable places. A key to deep relationships is reciprocity. However, it takes time, trust, and a willingness to genuinely open up to a person. Because of vastly different upbringings, degrees of trauma experienced, and levels of trust, you, and those you enter into relationships with are likely to have differing vantage points. So, you need to feel secure before you open up to friends and love interests.

Here are some good questions to help you discern a person's trustworthiness.

- "Do they follow through?"
- "When you call and leave a message, do they call back?"

- "Do they spend time with you, and are you willing to spend time with them?"
- "If you need something, do you feel comfortable asking them to fulfill that need?"
- "Would they be a good emergency contact?"

You can nurture your relationships when you take time to ask friends, family, and partners about the primary way they feel seen and loved. When you give them focused attention in these ways, they tend to reciprocate with lovingkindness. Without knowing what makes people feel loved, you most likely think they feel valued similarly to how you feel loved. Instead of assuming people feel loved and treasured in the same way you do, get curious about what makes others truly happy. Ask good questions instead of making assumptions because presuming can lead to misunderstanding and disappointment.

You may wonder what developing good communication skills has to do with walking the path toward enlightenment. It has everything to do with it because when you are caught up in stories and drama from the past, you become a pawn of the ego. Have you harbored hostility toward a parent from childhood into adulthood? How have your work relationships been damaged because of a lack of communication? How often have you asked yourself why you can't connect with your partner or children? How much life energy do you expend listening to your run-on thoughts about how things aren't the way you want them to be? How much anger, hurt, and resentment are trapped in your body? When you give negative thoughts unwarranted energy, they trigger emotions. These thoughts and feelings are common along life's journey, so recognizing their transient nature becomes a life practice.

Keep a keen eye out when feeling imprisoned by suppressed resentments. It will weigh you down and tether you to ego. Words unspoken and feelings harbored are felt by your loved ones, too. But when you clean up grudges and hurts by calmly discussing them or seeking counseling to explore them, your heart opens to genuine connection. So, remember to engage the Watchful Observer and bring awareness to thoughts and feelings as they float by. You can choose to shift your focus away from what you feel is lacking and foster what you want to cultivate. Focus with eyes of lovingkindness. When we learn to give to others the exact thing we think we're not getting, room is created for magic to happen.

Clarifying Questions

Some questions elicit only a "yes" or "no," answer, which doesn't encourage meaningful conversation, deep under-standing, or help to clarify. The questions that lead to yes and no answers begin with "is," "are," "do you think," and "should." But as I mentioned earlier, when you focus on open-ended questions, you will solicit thoughtful, insightful answers. These questions begin with "who," "what," "when," "where," "why," and "how."

Clarifying questions are follow-up questions that tend to evoke more profound and more revealing answers. You can ask the person you're speaking with to give an example of what their answer meant. For example, if someone says, "I just don't think that's fair," you can ask, "What exactly do you mean by fair?" or "Why do you think they are not being fair?" Do not interrupt while that person responds. If you are uncertain that you don't understand what they said, repeat it back to them. Start with,

"If I understand you correctly, you are telling me you're hurt because I didn't include you in the discussion before I made a decision." Also, remaining silent after asking a question allows the person to land on a revealing answer.

When I was pregnant, my then-husband and I took a parenting class, and our instructor gave this example of miscommunication that opened my eyes. A father asked his son to clean their garage. The child dutifully carried out his father's request. Later, the dad went to the garage expecting to see it clean, but when it wasn't, he yelled, "I said clean the garage. It's still a mess! Why didn't you do what I asked?" The upset child responded, "I did clean the garage. I moved my bike and picked up the trash."

The father hadn't clearly stated what he expected his son to do, so he reacted emotionally when he realized the son hadn't met those expectations. Dad's emotional response didn't help the child understand those expectations. Neither the child nor the dad learned from this communication. The dad remained angry, and the child remained confused. Clear communication and asking good questions could have alleviated a harsh exchange that caused alienation and hurt. This kind of misunderstanding creates the hurt that shapes belief systems, erodes self-esteem, and makes us feel isolated and disconnected from others. Unfortunately, these miscommunications happen daily with our children, partners, friends, and co-workers.

Expectations

Expectations are fertile soil to grow disappointments and mis-communications. When you bring awareness to the mind's wandering and your conversations, you'll sometimes notice that you hope to get a need met. But when you are attached to a specific outcome, you set yourself up to suffer emotionally if that need isn't met.

When I became aware of the minefield of expectations, I took an inventory of my life to find situations in which my expec-tations caused unnecessary suffering. One encounter almost ended my relationship with my mother. About thirty years ago, my husband and I wanted to borrow money from her, a one-year loan with interest, to build our home. I left home at 17 years old and had not asked for anything from my parents until this request. My mother had loaned each of my brothers the same amount of money I was requesting, so I went into the conversation expecting that she would at least entertain our proposal out of fairness.

She abruptly cut me off when I brought up the request and told me she wasn't a bank. My response was immediate and uncharacteristic, given my personality. I stood up and started barking orders at my husband. "Get our son and all our stuff and pack the van." We were visiting from out of town, and I couldn't get out of that house fast enough. I was angry be-cause she cut me off and had no desire to listen to me. And I was hurt because she had listened to my brothers when they asked to borrow money for their businesses. I remember throw-ing our suitcases out the door and having every intention of driving away and never returning.

My mother asked me to sit by the pool with her to talk. She told me she was selfish because she was an only child. I appreciated her honesty and didn't ask why she loaned my brother's money or why she didn't even want to hear our business proposal. I knew my desire to be heard was never going to be met. My expectation was causing my suffering. I realized at that moment I had two choices: to end my relationship with my mother or to continue my relationship *and* never expect anything from her, not even to be heard. I flashed forward in my mind to the last days of her life and knew I didn't want her to die alone; I wanted to be with her, holding her hand.

I decided to stay in our relationship and immediately released my expectations and anger. Not once after this did I ever have another expectation of her. Later in life, when Alzheimer's washed away even her selfishness, I gave my mother the love and security that I anticipated I wanted to give all those years in the past. I held her hand when she died.

Embrace Your Curious Nature

Curiosity is part of our genetic makeup but becomes buried under the weight of our socialization process. We are born curious. For example, children learn by witnessing cause and effect. As they interact with the world surrounding them, their main question is, "Why?" As parents, we surely remember our sheer exhaustion from answering our kids' steady stream of questions. But when children enter public school, it becomes impossible for a teacher to answer all the "whys" from thirty students. The learning process becomes one of memorizing answers to specific questions, where kids are rewarded with good grades for answering accurately. They begin to shy away from asking questions for fear of looking stupid and uncertain.

To grow in wisdom on the path to enlightenment, curiosity is the most essential personality characteristic to cultivate because the process of questioning awakens us to the illusion of the ego. It's equally as important to ask yourself good questions as it is to ask others. Not only will you get to know people better when you ask engaging questions, but you will also get to know yourself better. Asking questions helps you to be less self-centered or self-conscious. You become more interested and interesting. Neurons light up in the brain when you ask a question, and when you ask engaging questions, you become solution-oriented instead of problem-focused.

A dear friend of mine was having an issue with a longtime friend and she reflected on how her friend's behavior affected her and how she felt. Her friend also recognized a bump in their relationship, but neither knew how to find a solution. Now, my friend is not only dear but also wise, and she came up with this question for her friend: "What is my part in this?" This brilliant question invited engagement without eliciting blame or defensiveness. What a magnificent way to shift the energy in a positive direction. "What is my part in this?" is also a brilliant question to ask yourself often.

When you feel prickly because of something someone says, it's you who's feeling prickly. This is because a past unresolved incident is being re-stimulated or challenging a belief you think you need to defend. When you view your reactions as a mirror to learn from, you will grow in awareness and emotional intelligence. You will get better at responding to life situations instead of reacting with raw emotions that often aren't related to the current situation.

Don't Expect People to Read Your Mind – Tell Them

A question like, "What is my part in this?" coming from a loving, curious heart is a game-changer. So often, when we experience conflict, we tend to blame others or fear we will be blamed. We tend to want to be right. We can build elaborate justifications for our position and vehemently defend our emotional hurts. When we do this, our thinking becomes obsessive, and peace of mind and happiness evades us. There is no room for curiosity here.

Here are some questions you can ask yourself when faced with conflict, when you have a decision to make, or when you want to explore your thoughts or feelings.

- What is my part in it?
- Does this decision serve my life mission?
- What is the thought that caused this feeling? Is it true?
- Is there a more creative solution?
- What is a better question?
- Am I trying to be right?
- What outcome am I attached to?
- What could be easier? More fluid?
- What opinions do I have about this situation?
- Do I want to spend my energy this way?
- Does this make me happy?
- Am I being controlling?
- Am I taking this personally?
- What would happen if I wiped the slate clean?

- Does this current situation remind me of something that happened in my past?
- Is my reaction similar to what I witnessed in one of my parents? Caregivers?
- What would be my advice if I watched someone else engaging in this conflict I'm involved in?

Make asking open-ended questions a priority when you want to know people better or foster authentic communication and intimacy. When you feel you aren't connecting with people or want a deeper relationship, you can overemphasize your wants and needs. Instead, set an intention to hear the person with whom you want to connect. Let your needs take the back burner and get curious about what makes this person tick. Before conversing, ask yourself, "Am I willing to communicate with an open heart and mind? Am I willing to be wrong? Have I let go of my expectations? Am I willing to compromise?"

Questions to ask someone when you want to know them better and to foster deeper communication and intimacy:

- Who was your favorite childhood friend?
- What's on your bucket list if you have one?
- Which relative did you feel closest to?
- How do you feel about change?
- What do you fear most?
- How does it stop you from doing something you want to do?
- If you could go anywhere in the world, where would it be? Why?
- If you started a non-profit organization, what would it be?

- How do you feel about talking about dying?
- What do you most want to avoid?
- What quality do you value most in people?
- If you could invite anyone in the world for dinner, who would it be?
- What topic excites you most?
- What does it look like when you're in touch with your creative energy?
- What is the scariest thing you've ever done?
- What is the most adventurous thing you've ever done?
- What was your relationship with athletics in school?
- How did you feel about learning in school?
- What do you believe about being eternal beings?
- What is the most exciting or enjoyable vacation you've ever been on?
- What quality do you possess that you hope people recognize in you?

Questions to ask each other to build intimacy:

- What do you want me to know?
- How do you see me?
- Is there anything you are afraid to tell me?
- What have I done that you feel happy about?
- What have I done that you feel angry about?
- What could we do together that you'd find exciting?
- What are our strengths?
- What issues do you think we need to work on?
- What qualities attracted you to me?
- What did you learn from your parent's relationship?
- What is your favorite memory of us?
- How can we foster more humor in our relationship?

- What can I do for you that would make you feel appreciated?
- What could I do that would make your life easier?
- What are you most thankful for in our relationship?
- Are there things you want to do for yourself that you're not doing?
- How can we grow closer?

Five Whys Exercise

Below is a method I was introduced to and have used with profound results. Originally known as Five Whys, it can be used to determine the root cause of a problem. When I first used the exercise, I needed seven whys to get to the heart of the matter. You can use this exercise to solve problems, determine your deep motivations, or see what holds you back from your heart's desire.

The process is simple. Pose the first question. Answer it. Then, reframe your answer as a question, which will now be question number two (see my example below). Continue in this manner for questions three through seven. The last step is to formulate a corrective action. I prefer to call this step a *healing* action. To do this, create a mantra that contradicts the hurt and moves you closer to what lights you up. If the exercise led you to the realization that anxiety prevents you from moving forward, a healing mantra would be, "I am calm and relaxed."

Here's what the exercise looked like for me. I began with this statement, "I want to finish my book on enlightenment and become a speaker to share the book's teachings."

What I thought was a benign, non-emotional statement brought me to a very emotional ending at the completion of the exercise. I realized: "I didn't feel good enough, and if I stayed distracted, I didn't have to feel the pain. When an event makes me feel this way, I can stay with the feeling and say, I am enough. I am not distracted; I am totally present."

I listed my questions and answers so you can see how the process evolved for me. While doing this, tears started to flow at question number six, and I was sobbing at number seven.

1. Why do you want to finish your book on enlightenment and become a speaker to share the book's teachings?
   Because I want to help people live more creative, happier lives.

2. Why do you want people to lead more creative, happier lives?
   The more aware people are, the more conscious the world will be.

3. Why do you think more aware people will make a more conscious world?
   We bring on much of our own suffering because we lack the tools to shift our consciousness from ego to divinity.

4. Why do you think we cause most of our own suffering and lack the tools to shift our consciousness from ego to divinity?
   Because we are stuck in our egos and don't nurture our spirits.

5. Why do you think we are stuck in our egos and don't nurture our spirits?
   Because we are wounded and try to fill our wounds with distractions.

6. Why do you think we are wounded and try to fill our wounds with distractions?
    Because I am wounded and try to fill my wounds with distractions.

7. Why are you wounded, and why do you fill your wounds with distractions?
    Because I don't feel good enough, and if I stay distracted, I don't have to feel the pain.

Remember, emotions are like waves of energy in the body. When you release an emotion when reacting to an external event in the environment, the chemical reaction takes about 90 seconds to move through you. You can breathe into it, and then it will pass. But when you suppress that energy, it gets locked in the body. Remember the importance of releasing blocked emotions to open the channels of divine energy.

What is the Difference Between Pain and Suffering?

There is profound wisdom in an ancient Buddhist saying, "Pain is inevitable; suffering is optional."

When an event happens, distinguishing pain from suffering helps alleviate unnecessary suffering and leads to a happier life. Emotions are the instant brain response to an uncontrollable event that happens to us. The brain region involved in the experience of physical pain overlaps with some of the same areas that control emotional pain. The loss of a loved one, a broken heart from being jilted by a lover, being hurt in a car accident, or getting robbed are all painful experiences of the human condition. Suffering is then the story we make up about the painful event. It is a resistance to the pain instead of acceptance of the experience of pain. Emotional and physical pain will move through the body and release over time. But the story about the pain can keep one suffering for days, weeks, years, and lifetimes.

In the Release Your Pain – Embrace Your Power exercise, you excavated your past detrimental, repetitive stories and released them and the blocked emotions that weighed you down. Daily life events will continue to bring new traumas, challenges, and situations that push buttons and make you feel reactive. Triggers also will continue to bring on emotional reactions from the past, but you *can* choose how to respond to these situations as they come.

How to Make a Conscious CHOICE

Below are two scenarios describing the same event. One event ends in suffering, and one event ends in healing. By choosing how you respond, you can change the event's outcome.

Scenario One – Event + Pain + Story about the Event = Suffering

Event

A friend you've had for decades sends you an e-mail to break off your relationship.

Pain

As you read the e-mail, your heart begins to beat faster. Waves of energy move through your body, and tears well up. You feel out of control and rejected.

Reaction

You begin to pace. You pick up the phone to call her but immediately hang up. You go to the refrigerator and grab a beer. Thoughts start to swirl in your mind.

Story

"I am infuriated. I can't believe she did that. She couldn't even call to tell me. She is so insensitive. I've always been the giver, and she's been the taker. I am always the one who reaches out, and she didn't even call when my mother died. She doesn't care about me."

Then, you make a mental score sheet of all the times she has let you down. Later that evening, you mask the pain with any number of addictions and/or distractions. You wake up in the middle of the night, review the same storylines, and add some new ones. The following day, you call a confidant to rehash the story.

Scenario Two – Event + Experiencing the Pain = Emotional Release

Event

A friend you've had for decades sends you an e-mail to break off your relationship.

Pain

You read the e-mail. Your heart begins to beat faster. You feel waves of energy move through your body. Tears well up. You feel out of control and rejected.

Action

How to experience the pain:

- Feel the emotion in your body. Is your heart pounding? Is your throat closing? Are there knots in your stomach? Are your muscles tight? Is your mind racing?
- Sit down. Breathe into the places in your body where you feel the emotions. Name the emotions in an impersonal way. "This is fear. This is shame. This is anger."
- Accept the emotion...stay with it. Know that the emotions will quickly move through you and then pass.
- Learn from the experience – when you are no longer emotionally charged, explore what lessons your experience offers. Ask good questions, like "Why did I feel verbally attacked?" to reveal what deep hurt might have triggered the event.
- If you did make up a story about the event, reflect on the story. Use the reflection as a mirror so you can ask brave questions. For example, in Scenario One, I said my friend didn't care about me. So, I can use the reflection to see if there is anything that I accused her of that is true about me. I can ask myself, "Do I truly care about my friend? Is she always the taker, or are there times when she has been the giver?"

Questions Break Through the Story

Is it Hard to Wake Up?

In this material world, each of us gives meaning to words, objects, events, and interactions with others. When we infuse meaning into something, thoughts and opinions begin to form, *which* will then stir feelings. Because we give life meaning, we can also choose to change the beliefs and perceptions that accompany it.

If you remember, in Trail Marker 3, I described the process of re-framing as a therapy technique that provides a different way of looking at a situation, person, belief, or relationship. You can use that technique here if you keep telling yourself that waking up and gaining greater awareness is hard. So, to reframe that thought, say, "I am ready to take on the challenge of waking up. I will approach waking up with humor and curiosity."

In Trail Marker 8, I will share more about using tools like the image of a kaleidoscope to change your view of a situation, but for now, think about looking through a kaleidoscope and seeing a fixed scene inside. If you were to turn the kaleidoscope just one degree, an entirely different scene would appear. Reframing is like turning a kaleidoscope.

Your desire to wake up might not be greater than your desire to stay asleep, but with slight shifts, you will begin to savor the freedom that greater awareness offers. There is a phrase many alcoholics use to describe why they chose to give up drinking: "I was sick and tired of being sick and tired." What is making you sick and tired? When I was so disconnected from my spiritual self in my early twenties, I was sick and tired of being self-obsessed. I was sick and tired of trying to change my eating habits and being defeated by food. I was sick and tired of being stunted by perfectionism. I was sick and tired of feeling that I had more to offer the world while clueless about my life's mission. I was sick and tired of the constant voice of a bully inside my head. I was suffering, yet I knew in my bones that my thinking was responsible for the limited vantage point from which I was viewing my life. I also knew that the key to freedom and happiness was within me.

Remember, questions break through the story. Now, instead of debating concepts like hard or easy, or never questioning beliefs cemented in our minds, we can ask ourselves questions.

- "Does the belief, opinion, event, or interaction weigh me down or light me up?"
- "Does it feed the ego, or is it in alignment with a spiritually aligned life?"
- "Am I moving in the direction of fear or love?"

I've also come to understand how our reaction to life events can help us access what we need to do to wake up to our divinity. So please put on your dancing shoes and energy dance with your emotions, mind, body, and spirit. Just as it takes discipline and perseverance to learn to dance, living a mindful life also requires those qualities. I encourage you to find the sweet spot of effortless effort on the path to your awakening. As your true nature surfaces, you will flow with life instead of fighting and struggling with it. Breathe into the concept of effortless effort, and life's dance becomes more fluid.

The good news is you don't have to exert endless amounts of discipline and perseverance to awaken. Just as changing any behavior is the most challenging initially, developing awareness is, too. But once you practice gaining distance from your thoughts, feeling your pain instead of avoiding it, and recognizing stories when the mind constructs them, being aware will be your default.

In Trail Marker 7, I'll show you ways to fertilize your soul's garden to enrich your life. The mindfulness practices I offer teach you how to observe negative thought patterns. When draining, repetitive behaviors are illuminated, and as you divert your attention from them, you will see that they fade. You can also choose soul-affirming experiences instead of energy-depleting ones, continually practicing releasing what weighs you down and moving toward what lights you up!

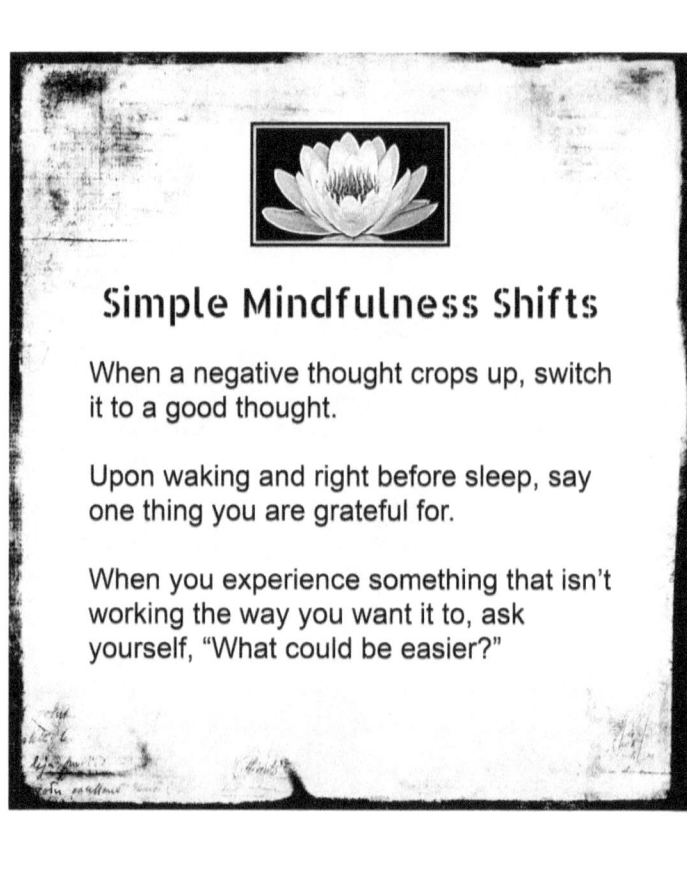

Simple Mindfulness Shifts

When a negative thought crops up, switch
it to a good thought.

Upon waking and right before sleep, say
one thing you are grateful for.

When you experience something that isn't
working the way you want it to, ask
yourself, "What could be easier?"

The Fifth Shift
Nourish Your Body, Mind and Spirit

> "If the only prayer you said was 'thank you,' that would be enough."
>
> – Meister Eckhart

Everything we do either nourishes or drains us, feeds our ego or inner life, and moves us toward love or fear. In this chapter, we keep in mind the interconnectedness of the body, mind, and spirit and do things that nourish us on our spiritual journey.

A well-nourished body, mind, and spirit is attuned to experiencing the flow of universal energy, the oneness of everything. As we gain distance from the distractions of our outer life, we focus on cultivating conditions for a calm and vital body, positive and affirming thoughts, and a happy and peaceful spirit. I'll show you how to enter a drama-free zone, develop a gratitude practice, slow down life's pace, discover simplicity's freedom, and learn how to add buoyancy to your life by infusing your day with laughter.

The more you intentionally feed your body, mind, and spirit, the less likely you are to fall prey to bad habits, self-sabotaging behavior, and mentally living in past and future thoughts. The ego, the mind-created self, relies on keeping you focused on fears, obsessions, and petty desires so that it can survive. But you can calm the ego by shifting your attention so its voice is a whisper, not a roar.

You can also weed out ego trappings and plant the thoughts, attitudes, and actions that nourish you. Simply observe. With eyes of awareness, moment by moment, recognize the numerous ways you can fortify your headspace with positivity and expand your heart with lovingkindness. Negative thoughts will recede when you do, and good thoughts will replace limiting fear-filled ones. Then, when the cunning ego demands your attention, you will no longer be a mindless pawn.

You will watch the ego at work, tirelessly vying for your attention. As the light of awareness illuminates the ego's deception, your sense of separateness will come into question – so will your beliefs. And you will realize there is more to life than can be experienced from a limited vantage point. When this happens, *Roadmap to Ease* will be here to guide you. You will read the simple mindfulness and lifestyle shifts below and then answer the questions after each section. As you answer the questions, ask yourself if this area in your life needs work or if you think all is harmonious in this area.

Choose Good Thoughts

Because we are wired to think negatively and beliefs are cemented once they form, switching from negative thought loops to positive thoughts takes practice. To begin, simply observe thoughts without judgment. This practice reveals the ever-changing nature of thoughts, which helps you be-come aware that *you are not your thoughts*. But sometimes, the voice in your head can be thunderous, and you've been conditioned to robotically give it attention, so simply watch-ing your thoughts may seem impossible. But when you're stuck and tightly wound with fear, anxiety, and worry, shifts such as choosing good thoughts to gain awareness and calm the mind are tremendously helpful.

Here's how my a-ha moment helped me rewire my brain's negativity bias. The idea of choosing good thoughts over bad thoughts sprung from a painful experience during a time when my son was abusing substances and living life on the wild side. He ran into a tree while driving drunk, escaping just before the car went up in flames. I witnessed the fire. Because of his abusive lifestyle, my mind was continually filled with fear-ful thoughts, and I was constantly waiting for the phone to ring with bad news about my son. Consequently, I was living in a state of stress, worry, and tremendous suffering caused by my fear-laden thoughts.

Later, I found my way to an Al-Anon meeting. A gentleman spoke about the hard time he had with his son and real-ized it was easier for him to replace bad thoughts with good thoughts. A light bulb went on in my brain, and I decided then and there to choose good thoughts about my son moving for-ward. I realized that most things I had worried about didn't happen. This shift in my thinking influenced a change in my son. As I worked on releasing my fear and letting go of always thinking the worst would happen, I was taking care of myself and wasn't micromanaging his life. There was a correlation be-tween me letting go of fear and my son taking responsibility for his well-being. Both of our lives turned in powerful ways, and the lessons I learned then contributed to forming my business, *Choose Good Thoughts*.

A wonderful Cherokee Indian tale called *The Legend of Two Wolves* brilliantly describes the conflict between choosing to think good thoughts or bad thoughts. In this legend, a wise grandfather uses the metaphor that two wolves are fighting within him to explain the nature of inner conflict to his grandson.

He says, "I have a fight going on inside me. It's between two wolves. One wolf is arrogant, angry, filled with envy, and feels superior. He stews with resentment, false pride, and regret. The other wolf is peaceful, loving, kind, generous, and filled with hope, compassion, and faith. This fight is also going on within you and in every person.

The grandson paused and asked his grandfather, "Which wolf will win?"

The grandfather responded, "The one I feed."

As I've mentioned, most of your thoughts today are the same ones you had yesterday, so they are easily recognizable. Chances are they have been with you for a long time. When a thought pops up, the first attempt is to let the positive or negative thought simply float by. Ultimately, we don't attach to passing thoughts on the path to enlightenment. But sometimes, we can't get distance from our relentlessly punishing thoughts. When this happens, mindfully replace the bad or negative thought with a good or positive thought. For example, "I will never get everything I need to accomplish done today." You can reframe this energy-draining thought: "I have all the time in the world to accomplish everything I need to do. What doesn't get done can wait."

Imagine a negative thought pattern that is stored in the subconscious mind like a record needle stuck in its groove, repeatedly playing the same few lyrics. The process of contradicting a negative thought pattern isn't as easily done as lifting a needle off a record and it doesn't happen overnight. Still, I can guarantee that if you continually weed out the annoying and sometimes paralyzing thoughts from your mind's garden and plant good thoughts, you will be rewarded with a quieter, happier mind. Then, the next step, simply watching your thoughts, will be easier for you.

Ask Yourself...

- Do I get stuck in negative thought loops?
- Are most of my thoughts today the same thoughts I had yesterday?
- Do I recognize when I am lost in thought that I can shift and watch my thoughts?

Drama-Free Zone

Entering a drama-free zone is consciously deciding not to engage in dramatic discourse and intentionally separating your life from drama. It takes vigilance to develop a keen sense of self-awareness to recognize all the ways we can get caught up in unnecessary drama. Still, you get sucked into some dramas, and others you create yourself. But to craft a happier, more creative life, there is no room for drama. Drama drains your energy, and as you know, creativity doesn't flow where energy is blocked.

Self-created drama usually arises when you think something is true and it's not. When you misinterpret the words or actions of friends, a spouse, children, or co-workers and fail to ask them to clarify, you are likely to begin an internal dialogue based on a misconception. You can also create drama when you think people will negatively react to an issue, even though you don't know if this is true. You skate around subjects or entirely avoid topics to dodge anticipated reactions. So, recognize when you are headed down these dark and twisty drama-laden paths. Correct the situation by openly communicating with those involved in the "drama" to gain clarity.

I fabricated a drama recently. It's amazing how much mental energy I wasted and how many elaborate stories I concocted to justify my case. My brother and I inherited a beautiful cottage in Maine, which has been in the family since my birth. Our families adored summers at the lakefront paradise. I'd felt the financial and logistical weight of owning a property so far from my hometown, but I didn't want to address the possibility of selling the cottage with my brother because I was sure he would react negatively.

After months of deliberation, I realized two issues – the challenges of owning a property so far away and the expense of cottage upkeep. When I finally called my brother to discuss the matter, he said he understood and had similar issues with cottage ownership. The moral of the story is to address problems when they arise. The only caveat is to state the issues concisely and respond calmly. If I had approached my brother with the negative case I built in my mind to justify my position before removing my emotional charge, our conversation would not have gone well. My story made things way too personal, bringing in unnecessary details that would only end in hurt feelings.

Store check-out lines can be sites for dramatic displays of angry outbursts and constant complaining. How often have you been standing in line to make your purchase when the person behind you is fuming about the slow-moving line? They want you to commiserate to help justify their upset. Once you become mindful of this kind of drama, you can choose not to engage in negativity. When I'm in a store line, and this happens, I infuse the situation with levity and engage the person in a drama-free way.

If their complaint is a slow-moving line, I might say, "Sounds like you have something wonderful to do today, and you're in a hurry to get there." Most of the time, the person's mood shifts immediately, and we start a pleasant conversation.

When my son was a preteen, we often got into dramas. The situation usually arose when he was nagging me for something I didn't want him to have. The arguments would leave me exhausted and feeling inadequate as a mother, and they would leave him angry or frustrated.

Eventually, though, we talked about the dramatic, cyclic pattern we were engaged in. I had the idea to choose a word to say whenever either of us felt emotionally charged and were not clearly communicating. We chose "switch," and it worked like a charm. When either of us said the word it elicited levity and created ease around our entangled energy. We'd effortlessly discuss our points of view and learn from the interaction. It helped our relationship stay in a drama-free zone, and, to this day, when the word "switch" comes up in a conversation, we laugh and remember how a simple shift made such a big difference in our ability to communicate effectively. When there is stuck energy, it's always a perfect opportunity to use your ingenuity to shift the energy.

Ask Yourself...

- Was there a lot of drama in our house when I was growing up?
- Do I make up stories in my head that might be constructed from expectations, perceptions, or opinions?
- Can I step back from the dramatic story in my head and observe it?

Infuse Life with Laughter

Who doesn't like a good belly laugh? Make laughter a priority. Laughter invigorates you physically and mentally, decreases stress hormones, and releases endorphins, the feel-good chemical. Physically, you take in more oxygen when you laugh, improving your immune system. Laughter elevates your mood and creates a positive state of mind. Laughter makes strong human connections. I suggest taking a mental inventory of how much you laugh. Think about which friends you are silly around. When was the last time you belly laughed? Plan uplifting adventures weekly that elicit laughter; watch silly movies, play board games that make you giggle, buy hula hoops for the kids (and don't forget one for yourself!), or have a water balloon fight. Make it your mission to experience belly laughter and create the circumstances that invite laughter.

And yes, there are always serious issues in the world that will dominate your thoughts and conversations. You can get very concerned, angry, and downright fearful if you absorb a steady diet of social media or the news. We all feel a full spectrum of emotions, but because we're wired to focus more on the negative than the positive, it's important to remember laughter is good medicine and the antidote for taking life, or ourselves, too seriously. A stellar way to become more buoyant as you travel life's journey is to learn to laugh at yourself.

Saint Thomas Moore said, "Happy are those who laugh at themselves because they will never stop having fun."

When you quit judging yourself and accept who you are, you detach from others' opinions about you. You become as kind and loving to yourself as you are to others. It takes self-acceptance to laugh at yourself. When you learn not to take things personally, you will experience a deep inner peace and approach life more light-heartedly.

Ask Yourself...

- Was there a lot of laughter in my home growing up?
- Do I consider myself light-hearted or serious?
- Do I find it easy to laugh at myself when I've made a mistake?

Embrace Change

My grandpa often told me, "There is nothing constant but change."

When I was a young child, I didn't understand the magnitude of his words. When we observe the natural world, we witness constant change. Being fluid is quite difficult for some of us, and accepting life as it unfolds can seem utterly impossible. And yet, until you accept what can't be changed, you suffer – we all do. Change can also make you feel threatened. If you've lost a job, been left by a partner, or are a victim of a natural disaster, you experience emotions ranging from terror to profound sadness and despair.

The Serenity Prayer offers a great mantra to deal with change: "Grant me the serenity to accept the things I cannot change, the courage to change the things I can, and the wisdom to know the difference."

When you observe each life situation, you can gain the wisdom to know what aligns with your soul and makes you happy. You can also recognize when you put yourself through unnecessary suffering because you continually try to change the things that can't be changed. We can't bring our loved ones who have passed away back. We can't make people love us even if we are madly in love with them. As you grow in wisdom, your life will become easier when you focus on changing those things that *can* be changed and not focusing, sometimes for months or years, on things that can't be changed.

Ask Yourself...

- When I was young, was there a lot of change in my life, schools, homes, caregivers, and how did it affect me?
- What are the times in my life when I didn't embrace opportunities because of my fear of change?
- How does change affect me now?

Simplify Your Life

Everyday chores and the endless details of daily life can be performed robotically or with mindfulness. Your to-do list will remain until your dying day. As long as there is breath in your body, there will be bills to pay, cars to fix, food to gather and prepare, clothes to wash, and body maintenance to manage. When you have children living at home, it involves more daily chores and responsibilities. And caring for aging parents is a time-consuming act of devotion.

If you belong to the 'sandwich generation,' you may even care for aging parents while supporting children. Getting around to self-care or fertilizing your soul's garden seems impossible for all these reasons and more, but happiness and satisfaction depend on making time for it. Studies show that our greatest joys comes from a rich family life, deep friendships, passion, purpose, and giving back to the world.

But some things can interfere with these greatest joys. 'Stuff' is one of them. Advertisements sell happiness disguised as new cars or dream vacations and can cause some people to desire what they don't have and can't afford. These conditions set a trap for distraction and dissatisfaction. Living in a capitalistic society, we can be bombarded with countless choices and have access to unlimited possessions, creating a tendency to accumulate stuff and lots of it.

Not everyone, of course, but undoubtedly, many continually aspire for bigger and better things. For example, if I have one child, then I want two. Next, I'll want a bigger house to have room for my growing family. Then, the bigger house needs more furniture and larger closets for more clothes and shoes.

The family now needs a minivan, not a sports car, and so on. I'm not saying that wanting more money or possessions is good or bad, right or wrong; I'm just cautioning you not to base happiness on acquiring stuff. And I cannot overemphasize the importance of being aware of *choice overload*. The more choices you have as a consumer, the greater the possibility you'll make a purchase.

I typed 'jeans' in the Amazon search bar, and over 10,000 choices came up. The last thing I needed was another pair of jeans, but I did click on a fabulous pair that popped up on the first page! Do you remember when there were only a few jean brand options? I do! Making decisions takes energy. When making an informed decision, there are many variables to weigh. The more choices you have, the harder it may be to decide. And when you finally choose, you are less likely to be satisfied with the choice than you would have been if you had fewer choices. This is because, with so many options, you can feel regretful, thinking you could have made a better decision.

So, how do you limit the time suck and energy drain that happens when you allow yourself to entertain too many choices? Here are my two useful shifts that will leave you happier, with more energy and a quieter mind.

First, *simplify your choices*. It's estimated that an individual makes about 35,000 decisions daily, and many of them are unconscious. This contributes to a lot of mind activity that will keep you in ego consciousness. Steve Jobs wore a black turtleneck shirt, blue jeans, and the same type of sneakers daily because he didn't want to expend extra energy making clothing decisions. To simplify your choices, make decisions ahead of time. After you have completed your day's work, plan a to-do list for the following day. But instead of compiling an endless to-do list, write down one 'must do' task and two 'other' tasks to complete. Put the thing you want to do least on the top of the must-do task. This is because you can spend much time and energy avoiding tasks you don't want to do. Avoidance distractions include searching the internet, watching funny animal videos, or making several trips to the fridge. Once you complete the task you were avoiding, you will experience freedom and ease for the rest of the day.

One of the ways I have simplified choices is my practice of eating healthy by eliminating bad food choices. I don't have to use my willpower or repeatedly decide to avoid fast food because decades ago, I chose not to eat fast food. I also decided never to use a vending machine, and when shopping for food, I don't buy sugar-filled items. Of course, there are exceptions to my rules, but they are few. Making choices one time, like not bringing sweets into the house and sticking to them, helps with conscious eating. I don't have to try to exert willpower over and over to resist eating treats because they aren't in the house.

Before deciding choices and poor food choices, I had an internal dialogue, battled to make healthy choices, and beat myself up when I continually made the wrong choice. Then, I started to pay attention to how I felt when I ate unhealthy foods, which helped me make better food choices. Now, I spend a few hours a week making beautiful, healthy foods to freeze. I don't exhaust myself with constant decision-making, have no shame for bad choices, and, most importantly, I don't have a war waging inside my head.

The second exercise I made up to simplify life is called the Get Rid of a 1,000 Things Challenge. This will lighten your life by purging items. These items can be anything you choose. For example, you can count each deleted email as one thing. Start with items that don't hold a strong attachment, like your junk drawer. Work your way up to your clothes, shoes, and jewelry. Everyone I know who has tried this challenge had a blast doing it. The lighter you feel, the easier it gets to purge unwanted items. Think about the people who might love your unwanted items and pass your once-treasured belongings along. Ideally, you'll go through all your belongings, and by the end of the purge, you'll be surrounded by items you love. An organized, curated space will make you feel happy, and the order will calm your mind.

As I review the past decades of my life, I see now some modifications would have created more ease, slowed down my mind, and inspired awe in the present moment. In a word, I could have *simplified*. So, instead of running toward the next shiny object, you can savor the simple things and find happiness in what you have. This simple shift in consciousness can help you appreciate the richness in your life.

Ask Yourself...

- Do I complicate my life? If so, how?
- Do I procrastinate? If so, how does it affect my life?
- What is one thing I can do that would simplify my life?

The Slow Movement

Examining how you move through the world is a steppingstone toward greater awareness. Before the Industrial Revolution, people were connected to their community, food, and cycles of life and death. They generally lived multi-generationally and in the same area for their entire life. The division of labor was based on need, not on aspiration.

For a community to eat, land had to be toiled, food had to be grown, and a bountiful crop relied on nature's cooperation. Meals were made from scratch. Clothing was hand-sewn. People were born and died at home. Life was not easy, but people were connected to each other, to nature, and to the cycles of life. But ever since the wheels of industrialization started turning, modern humans' daily activities have been on steroids. The ease with which we can relocate has scattered the family unit. The desire for everything to be fast and easy has spilled into every aspect of daily life.

The Slow Movement is a relatively new concept that advocates a cultural shift toward slowing down life's pace. It invites mindfulness into every aspect of life and offers the opportunity to focus on connections once again – our connection to ourselves, to each other, and to nature's rhythms. The more we spend time in nature, the more we realize our interconnectivity to everything. Ultimately, enlightenment is experiencing everything as one, to see beyond the illusion of separateness. When we take in the essence of a rose, we understand a rose isn't just a rose. The rose grew because of its dependence upon the sun, rain, soil, humidity, temperature, and nutrients. The rose is one with all these elements. When we slow down, we recognize our similarities to a rose since we both wouldn't survive without the same essential elements.

Slow Living

The intention to slow down can enter every aspect of your life. Just as you can utilize the Watchful Observer to disengage from thoughts, so can you become aware of your energy to observe how you move through the world. You can mindfully slow down when you recognize that you are moving too fast. Sometimes, we get a big wake-up call when we are moving too fast, mindlessly, or recklessly. My wake-up call rang when I drove off a 50-foot cliff in an MG Midget. Have you had a wake-up call?

How fast do you move through the day? Do you speed around like a marathon runner or keep the perfect pace, mindful of the present moment? Or are you a bit sloth-like, on the couch resting while your spirit would like to do something in alignment with your inner life? You might believe that if you do tasks at a faster pace, you will get more accomplished. This isn't necessarily true, but even if it were, there are huge costs of moving at the speed of light. When you move at 90 miles an hour long enough, you eventually feel overwhelmed, distracted, or exhausted. Fun and humor evade you, and your focus soon becomes the voice in your head narrating your every move. Your children, partners, and co-workers will also experience your rushed energy. Or maybe they won't notice because they are moving fast, too.

Unique markings on autumn's fallen leaves, a majestic heart-shaped cloud dancing across the sky, or the labored flight of an osprey carrying a huge branch can go unnoticed by hurried humans. Mindfully, you can shift your perspective from a human "doing" to a human "being." Slow down, be fully present, and savor *this* moment so that you can treasure its passing. Start where you are, observing how you move through your day. You won't go from marathon speed to chill overnight. To move slower and more mindfully, pay attention to your breath. With your attention, it will slow down naturally and bring you into the NOW.

Ask yourself…

- When I was little, did the movement in our house seem slow or rushed?
- How did the pace of everyday activities feel when I was young?
- Do I feel rushed to do my daily activities, or am I at ease and moving mindfully through the day?

Slow Food

Ask yourself, "What is my relationship with food? Is fast food my typical fare? Do I prepare food with my mind on the next task, or am I mindfully chopping veggies? Do I gulp down meals or savor the subtle flavors and textures? Do I stress eat at the refrigerator or slowly in the glow of candlelight using lovely dishes and cloth napkins?"

How and what you eat is not just about you; it's about your entire family. Your eating habits and relationship with food affect them as well. You can teach kids how food is grown, what regions it's grown in, its nutritional value, and how our consumption choices impact their bodies and the planet. Bringing the concept of slow food into your home keeps you in touch with the nourishment that fuels your body, as well as your family's.

Mindful eating improves your health and encourages family togetherness. You might even dust off old family recipes to replace ready-to-serve meals with a few made-from-scratch favorites. Slow cooking is reminiscent of bygone days when a bustling kitchen was the home's heart. So, rather than a rushed meal, having a lingering eating experience creates new family memories and time to talk about the day's happenings.

Ask Yourself...

- Did my family eat most of our dinners together at a specific time?
- When I was growing up, was mealtime a relaxed, happy time?
- Did my relationship with food when I was growing up affect my relationship with food now?

Slow Parenting

Many of our children have non-stop schedules, going directly from school to sports practice, piano lessons, or ballet class. Because this pace requires frequent driving, dinner ends up being fast food and on the go. Then, by the time you get home, the kids must complete school assignments for the next day. Weekends are often scheduled with multiple activities, too. This schedule leaves children little time to relax or find their inner rhythm. Practicing slow parenting means mindfully preserving time for children to unplug and enjoy unstructured time. Children may get bored. But left to their own imagination, kids figure out how to entertain themselves when parents don't jump in to alleviate the boredom. They get to explore life in their timing, not on a schedule.

When I was growing up, TV viewing choices were limited, and the internet did not exist. After school, all the neighborhood kids played outside until dinner and all day long during weekends. We were creative, built elaborate forts, swam for hours, played hide-and-seek, and rode our bikes to buy milkshakes. We looked out for each other. When someone was hurt physically or emotionally, we comforted one another. We formed an inseparable tribe, and many of us are still connected.

Studies suggest that eating together as a family has many benefits. A regular dinner time establishes a rhythm and a sense of belonging. Sharing family meals gives children a feeling of connection, making them less likely to suffer from anxiety. Family members keep in touch with one another and have opportunities for meaningful conversations, which can build a child's self-esteem. Having dinner 'chores' teaches the importance of shared responsibilities, instills self-discipline, and makes children feel capable, so let your kids participate in menu planning, cooking, and cleaning up.

You can ease into slow parenting. Begin by eliminating one weekly planned activity. Then incorporate any suggestions below that resonate:

- Commit to having a few meals together each week.
- Set aside a couple of hours for game time on weekends, like Monopoly, instead of sports on TV.
- Collect phones and put them away during 'family time.'

- Turn the TV off for an entire evening.
- Go for a family walk out in nature.
- Teach your children the skills and practices you are learning in this book.
- Help your children identify and express their feelings.
- Use quiet time in the evening to discuss communication skills and how to listen to one another.
- Start simple family rituals, such as saying one thing you are grateful for when you sit down for dinner.
- Buy a deck of Angel Cards (Google it) and have everyone pick a card before bed.
- Watch a feel-good movie together and discuss what you each learned from it or your favorite part.
- Discuss what you like about slowing down as a family and what you might want to do differently.
- Ask the children what they are learning from having a slower lifestyle.

Ask Yourself...

- Did I have a lot of quality time with my parents?
- Did I have family rituals, such as going to church, having multi-generational family meals one night a week, or going to the same vacation spot yearly?
- Did I feel I had too many extracurricular activities, not enough, or just the right amount?

Slow Travel

Have you ever felt like you need to take a vacation to recover from the vacation you just had? Maybe you have the family photos you took to document the moments, yet it's hard to recall the details. Did the smell of oven-fresh bread travel to your nose? Did you experience the grandeur of the Eiffel Tower with your eyes or observe it mainly through the lens of a video camera? When visiting new towns or countries, do you tend to stay in a hotel and fill your daily itinerary with back-to-back tourist activities?

Slow travel is about staying in an area for an extended period to explore the local culture, foods, crafts, and history. The next time you travel, consider renting a cottage or a room in a home. Take ambling walks, bike rides, and travel by subways or trains. Living like a local enables you to have a more intimate relationship with the town and the local people. Slow travel gives you the time and opportunity to experience an area with your senses, bask in the rhythm of the culture, and make connections on a deeper level than as a rushed tourist.

Ask Yourself...

- When I travel, do I like conversing with locals and learning about their communities?
- Do I savor moments when I travel, get out in nature, enjoy lingering meals, and mindfully ignore devices and social media?
- What pace do I keep when I travel? Is it comfortable, or would I like to change it?

Wisdom of the Body

Do you feel relaxed and at home in your body? In many surveys, when men, women, and even young teens are asked how they feel about their bodies, the vast majority use words like dissatisfied, unhappy, and negative. We formulate what an ideal body looks like from television, print ads, and social media platforms. Our socialization, mainly from the opinions of parents and caregivers, also dictates how we feel about our bodies. From an early age, often we were told what to eat, when we should eat, how we should look, and what we should weigh.

I recently found a picture of me in a Brownie uniform. My mother wrote on the back, "another fatty." She was most likely referring to herself as the other fatty. I was a little pudgy but certainly not fat, and my mother was never fat, either. This was a time when anyone ten pounds overweight was considered fat, at least in the circles where I grew up. From a young age, my internal monologue droned on about how I needed to lose weight. The negative self-talk created subconscious beliefs that consumed vast amounts of mental energy, resulting in abnormal eating behaviors and poor self-esteem.

When we have internalized issues like obsession with our weight, it becomes a problem we attempt to address with our mind. To achieve our desired results, I believe we quit tuning into our bodies and try to exert willpower to change our behavior. We can only resist for so long, and willpower gets depleted. When we attempt to use only willpower to achieve our desired outcome and fail, our internal messaging beats us up.

Instead of relying solely on willpower to change behaviors, utilize the body's wisdom. Let's stay with the desire to lose weight. When you go to the refrigerator for a snack, before you open the fridge, ask yourself on a scale of one to 10, "How hungry am I?" This question takes your attention away from the mind and focuses it on your body. Then, feel the degree of fullness or emptiness in your belly. Take a few deep breaths as you stay with the feeling. Give your body time to "tell" you its hunger level. Another helpful question to ask your body is, "What foods are the best nourishment for you?"

So, how do we learn to tune into our bodies and try not to control them with our minds? Develop a relationship between your mind, body, and spirit by tuning into their messages. First, breathe slowly and mindfully through your nose, feel the air expand your belly, then release your breath through your mouth. You are calming your mind and body with this gentle, rhythmic breathing. Do this at least five times. Now, put your hand over your heart and, using the same breathing technique, breathe into your heart five times as you bathe your body in love. Check in with your body, ask what it needs now, and listen until you hear the response.

Communicate with your body and spirit by asking, "What do I need to nurture my spirit? Are there any foods I should eliminate? Why is my body low in sodium?" If you don't get a response while doing this exercise, you may get an answer at another time, or it may come to you in a dream. Remember to shower your body, mind, and spirit with love and gratitude.

Ask Yourself…

- Is how I felt about my body in my younger years the way I now feel about my body?
- Do I check in with my body regularly and ask pertinent questions like, "Am I feeling anxious, tight, energetic, or exhausted?"

- Do I fill my spirit with things that light me up and make me feel centered and tuned into a spacious, peaceful place?

Live in Gratitude

Even though millions of acts of kindness are occurring worldwide at any given moment, news channels choose to report dire events instead. The mind can be like a news channel, hashing over all the things that might go wrong instead of focusing on the numerous things that go right. When our mind focuses on gratitude instead of what is wrong in life, it opens our hearts, improves our health, helps us manage stress, and so much more.

When looking at predictors of happiness, an attitude of gratitude ranks at the top of the list. When you make your gratitude list, rather than say or write the first thing that comes to mind when reflecting on life's gifts, dig deeper and think more creatively. A usual list might read something like, "I'm grateful for my daughter, my husband, and my art studio."

A more thoughtful and heart-opening list would be, "I am grateful for my daughter's sense of humor. She makes me laugh every day. My partner challenges me to be more adventurous. I love that he pushes my limits. I will never take my hands for granted. They enable me to do art that feeds my soul." Like some of the other practices and exercises I provide in *Roadmap to Ease*, developing an attitude of gratitude requires mindfulness and needs to be practiced daily until it becomes a natural part of your daily ritual.

Ways to Grow in Gratitude

Keeping a Gratitude Journal can be as simple as writing down three things you are grateful for each morning. You can also make weekly entries. If you wish, you can embellish your journal by adding drawings, photos, or doodles. Consider things you usually take for granted, like the wonder of eyesight or the blessing of bountiful food choices. Be sure to go back and read your journal entries each month. Reading your gratitude journal can be an uplifting, heart-expanding activity when you're feeling down.

Sprinkle 'Thank Yous' in Your Vocabulary by expressing gratitude often and sincerely, whether at home or out in the world. Look people in the eyes and express gratitude, letting them know they are seen and appreciated. During Covid, when I called a customer service rep and could hear their children in the background, I asked them how they were doing during those challenging times. We long for connection and simple acts of kindness can make the person we appreciate happy and make us happy, too.

Finding Gratitude in Adversity by not minimizing bad things that have happened. Feel the emotions that surface and let them move through you. Honor the healing process and realize healing takes time. If you've experienced significant loss, remember grief has stages we move through. Don't shortcut that process. Even when challenged, find gratitude for what you've gained by the challenge, like strength or wisdom. Passionate life missions have grown out of people's greatest adversities.

Ask Yourself...

- Was I brought up with a family that expressed gratitude?
- Do I have a gratitude practice or want to begin one?
- Am I a glass-half-full or a glass-half-empty type of person?

Practice Acts of Kindness

Buy coffee for the car behind you at the drive-thru. If you have something to teach, volunteer to share your wisdom at a local school or library or start a meet-up group. Let someone cut in line ahead of you. Send cards to children fighting a serious illness, individuals in nursing homes, or veterans in a VA medical facility. Pick up trash on the beach. Make a meal for a sick friend or offer a ride to a neighbor without a car. Make little gratitude cards and leave them in random places. Reach out to people from your past and tell them how much they still mean to you. Send an unexpected thank you card, a text, or an email. The simplest selfless acts of kindness can brighten someone's day and brighten yours, too.

Ask Yourself...

- Growing up, did I or my family practice acts of kindness?
- Did I teach my children to practice acts of kindness?
- When I think about performing acts of kindness, would I rather do things anonymously or give my time engaging with people face-to-face?

Gain the Wisdom

Albert Einstein said, "Wisdom is not a product of schooling but of the lifelong attempt to acquire it."

Historically, the goals of the public school system in America educate students to become active participants in a democratic society, help ensure the economic success of the country, and gain a competitive advantage in the marketplace. The system trains students to be compliant citizens and keeps the wheels of capitalism turning. Schools are often overcrowded and underfunded. Standardized teaching often prevents teachers from creating innovative curricula. Outdated learning methods and the program of studies don't foster creative expression and individual learning styles.

Students graduate with a diploma, but many have not developed a curious mind or a creative spirit. Basic life skills, like financial planning, effective communication, and emotional intelligence, are not addressed. Teachers focus on the skills that serve our outer life, the work world, and how to fit in society, which leaves students bankrupt in acquiring wisdom and missing an opportunity to cultivate a rich inner life.

Complex daily life situations come at us fast and furious, requiring an abundance of skills to stave off unnecessary suffering. We read all the parenting books and feel totally competent in our ability to be a loving parent. Suddenly, we give birth and are confronted with issues like postpartum depression, a colicky baby, and a partner who is constantly called out of town on business. Do not suffer alone and fall deeper into depression and fatigue. How do we call on wisdom in this situation? Reaching out for support is always a wise move. Phone a friend who has been through a similar situation and ask for help. Consult a doctor to address depression and tips for soothing a colicky baby.

The curve ball of life pitches us countless scenarios: a parent gets Alzheimer's, and you must care for them. You are diagnosed with a disease. Your best friend dies. Your company downsizes, and you're suddenly out of a job, or a hurricane hits your home. And then personal life situations arise, like coming to grips with behaviors you're exhibiting that no longer serve you. Maybe you recognize an unresolved childhood trauma, an eating disorder that's robbing your happiness, or a burning desire to embark on a creative endeavor. Still, you're frozen in fear or become paralyzed by perfectionism.

For all these situations, calling on wise counsel will provide the healing salve to calm your thoughts and relax your body. Instead of feeling overwhelmed by life's challenges, you'll reach out to people with a needed and helpful perspective or practice. Seeking our tribe, a community to feel connected, can be tremendously beneficial.

Facebook has lots of private groups that address very specific issues. Join groups and use your instincts when judging if the group offers solace and helpful information. Not all groups will feel like your tribe, so try several until one fits. You can find an array of inspirational and educational podcasts, TED Talks, and lectures featuring people dedicated to imparting wisdom. Many people share their greatest challenges with stunning authenticity and radical honesty. They have risen from dark places and shine light to illuminate the healing path. Their courage helps us see beyond our self-imposed limitations and become more fluid, braver, and attuned to our inner selves. Consider hiring a coach or mental health professional to assist your spiritual growth if you want one-on-one guidance.

Ask Yourself...

- Where do I feel stuck and need new information or insight to move past where I am?
- When I was a child, do I remember if my parents reached out for help when they were in stuck places?
- Do I feel I've spent as much time growing a rich inner life as I have cultivating a successful outer life?

Are you ready to acquire more tools to assist you on the path to greater ease and freedom? Trail Marker 8 provides an awareness toolkit chock-full of mindset shifts. Don't worry – you don't have to don a toolbelt to carry these instruments. They are imaginary tools you utilize by keeping the function of the tool and how it relates to your awakening in your mind. Trust me... it's easier than it sounds.

Spoiler alert: one of the tools is on the top five list of my favorite consciousness-shifting practices.

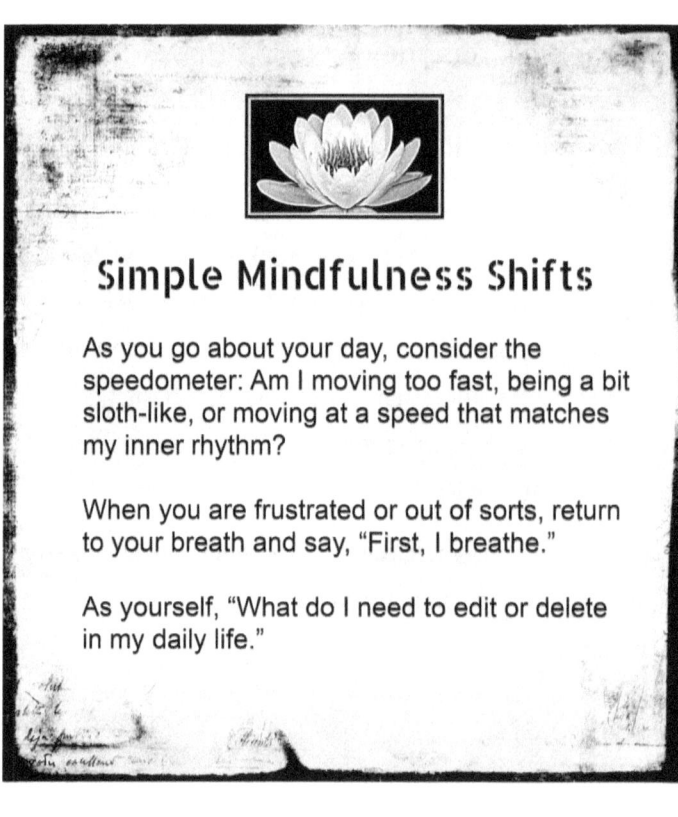

Simple Mindfulness Shifts

As you go about your day, consider the speedometer: Am I moving too fast, being a bit sloth-like, or moving at a speed that matches my inner rhythm?

When you are frustrated or out of sorts, return to your breath and say, "First, I breathe."

As yourself, "What do I need to edit or delete in my daily life."

The Awareness Toolkit

> *"Will my choice be in alignment with my commitment to a life of ease, freedom, and happiness?"*
>
> *– e'Layne Kelley*

My Inner Journey

As I addressed in Trail Marker 1, Waking Up to Your Divinity, my spiritual journey began in the mid-70s when I had several spiritual experiences, including a near-death experience that introduced me to an ever-present awareness.

My toolkit at that time was sparse, and I had no roadmap. While I had a deep desire at the time to delve into this awareness, my thoughts obscured my inner knowing. They were punitive, brutally so, and I felt like my life was purposeless. I desperately longed for relief from yo-yo dieting, obsessive thinking, self-medication, perfectionism, and seeking distractions.

My heart yearned for inner peace. My creativity, reverence, and self-acceptance, which I accessed easily as a child, stirred deep within me. But I could not bring them to the surface because of my fear of change, self-doubt, unworthy feelings, and guarded heart. Imprisoning thoughts dammed the flow of my creative energy, the light of divinity, and the quiet voice of intuition. The burden of unhappy thoughts felt all-consuming and too heavy to bear. I had no idea where to find the key to my freedom.

With no life purpose, I longed for clarity and happiness. Willpower wasn't enough to institute lasting changes, as I repeatedly tried and failed, believing that if I changed my outer world, found a life purpose, and had an ideal body, then I would be happy.

The first glimmerings of relief came when I began reading books about spirituality, Siddhartha, and Autobiography of a Yogi. Words on the pages lit up my heart, and it felt like I had come home. Embracing a spiritual longing and wanting to live the life of a seeker resonated within me. Slowly, my unyielding willpower morphed into a gentle yet passionate willingness to live with unanswered questions. When I stopped trying to figure things out intellectually, it freed me to take small steps that were in harmony with my heart. My ridged, perfectionist tendencies softened the more I leaned into gentle willingness.

In hindsight, I realized I had begun to do things that fed my soul. I exchanged my longing to have a different life for a life seeking inner guidance and direction. Walking the beach at sunset became a ritual. Meditation wasn't the easiest practice to develop, but I met my resistance with willingness and prayer. I kept showing up on my bench. As my mind quieted, I became less self-absorbed. These changes released blocked energy in my body and created feelings of space and calm. The freed energy seemed to match the universal energy I had experienced when I was young, and the sense of freedom and spaciousness was readying me for the next step of the journey, leaving the familiar behind.

As I shared in Trail Marker 1, while at The Abode, a message told me to leave my comfortable life at my Florida beach home and venture into the unknown. I followed my inner voice, and it led me to uproot my entire life and move to California. When I landed, no friends were waiting. I had no plan, no money, no job, or any ties to the area. For the first time in my life, I was without family or lifelong friends around me.

I wasn't the young girl whose father had died, the chubby, dutiful Catholic girl, the caretaking big sister, or the kid nick-named FBI, short for Frizbee Incorporated because I had wild hair. I was no longer known as the partying beach girl, the high school sorority girl, the public relations student at finishing school, the pool-shooting hard ass, or the pot-smoking, veg-gie-eating hippie. I was emptied of all I knew myself to be – a blank canvas. I had even left the name Elaine behind as Pir Vilayat, my Sufi teacher, had given me my spiritual name, Sakena, which means "peaceful and the inner life," a perfect meditation and focus for a new beginning.

Shortly after I arrived and found a place to live, I had an out-of-the-blue "aha moment." The sun was bright, and there was a slight nip in the air as I walked the streets of Walnut Creek toward the BART train station. The year was 1981, although I remember it like it was yesterday. Outfitted in rolled-up Army pants, Birken-stock sandals, and sparkly gold socks, I approached the train platform. Concentrating more on catching a ride to the city than enlightenment, I had this epiphany. We – everyone and everything on the planet – are one being. We are a drop in the ocean and also the entire ocean.

Pir Vilayat had imparted this teaching often, but at the time, it was just words. This particular day, on a BART train platform, I experienced it. I felt an even more profound "knowing" in my bones: the realization that we co-create everything with God, known by many names. I felt nothing was divisible. We are all one universal consciousness, and creativity is part of our spiritual DNA.

Standing before the blank canvas of my life, I learned firsthand what Confucius meant when he said, "And remember, no matter where you go, there you are."

I realized that until this concept is fully understood, it's easy to blame others or ever-unfolding life events for sabotaging dreams. The truth is we all have an opportunity to write and rewrite the story of our lives each minute of every day, no matter where we live and no matter what our life circumstances are. I also awoke to the realization that unencumbering myself from the things blocking my happiness is my responsibility.

I was introduced to spiritual teachers and therapy along my path, tending to inner wounds and limiting beliefs. Time in nature stirred awe and reverence in me. I continually questioned my beliefs, became a lifelong learner, gave voice to my creativity, and met dear, heart-centered friends. Gaining wisdom and feasting on spiritual truths began to fill a vast emptiness. In a few short years, I was unrecognizable as my former self. Being self-absorbed in addictive patterns and obsessive thinking about body image faded. I stopped attempting to extract a life's purpose from an empty vessel. Actions I would have considered risky in the past became adventures as I feared a little less in each moment. Seeds for ease, happiness, and spiritual growth were planted. I continued to fertilize previously barren soil attentively.

Awakening is a spiral path. I've had to negotiate boulders along it, big craggy ones. Often, my thoughts created the boulders. Other times, life situations, like grieving the loss of loved ones, divorce, or coming to terms with a life-threatening disease, tested my spiritual resolve. Sometimes sure-footed, sometimes stumbling, I awakened to the awareness that had been with me all along.

Once I stopped listening to the thunderous, negative voice that stimulated rote reactions and cavernous self-doubt, fear, and numbing indecision, they lost their grip on me. Looking back, I realize the journey from being a deer paralyzed in the headlights to a curious seeker walking the path to awakening changed my psychology. Now I understand that I no longer recognized myself because I was no longer the self that I had been. Though unbeknownst to me at the time, I see that stepping out of my fixed reality and negative mind into a world of new experiences *rewired my brain*.

Awareness is Needed for Change

Whether we realize it or not, we're all on a spiritual journey. Maybe you know you've been on an inner journey for a long time, or perhaps you're new to the discovery of awakening. No matter where you are on the path, if default patterns of behaviors are to change, you want to be vigilantly aware of two things. First, you need to be mindful of thoughts and behaviors that no longer serve you so you can work on rewiring your brain and avoid detrimental outcomes. Secondly, you hone your awareness to recognize when a situation elicits an eruptive feeling within you, and you're going to react ineffectively to a situation. When you are aware of emotional turbulence within, you can take a deep breath and calm yourself before you exhibit an inappropriate reaction. Tools in prior chapters, as well as the tools listed below, will help you fine-tune your awareness to mitigate negative thought loops and eruptive feelings. As they quiet, we move from ego domination to a spaciousness that brings us into the present.

Refraining from the mind's negative bias and building spiritual muscles requires rewiring the brain with a positive bias. Do you recognize a scenario like this? We get all jazzed up to start working out at the gym with visions of regained health, renewed self-control, and melting fat. The first few times, we're on track. Then muscles start burning, and getting to the gym as each day passes is harder. Negative thoughts stream in because of our subconscious wiring, especially when we don't see immediate results. Memories of money wasted over the years and times we gave up become more prevalent than memories of success. Staying in negative thought loops keeps us engaged in ego and walled off from our divinity.

We can rewrite our burdensome stories, but it takes shining the light of awareness on what we're doing and saying to ourselves. The tools below will help you become more aware, and rewiring the brain will change your behavior or belief.

Let's refresh the information we addressed in Trail Marker 2, Why Wake Up, on why the brain needs to be rewired and how to do it, so you have the concept of rewiring the brain fresh in your mind as you're introduced to these awareness tools below.

Neuroplasticity is the brain's ability to grow and change by forming new networks. In 1949, Donald Hebb discovered that "Neurons that fire together wire together." To get neurons to fire together and rewrite brain patterns, feeding the brain with new information, such as making art or learning a language, is the spark that facilitates this wiring. To create lasting change, you must do more than *think* about the change you want to make. It is essential to *feel* these new experiences in your body since experiencing feelings is the secret sauce that solidifies lasting change. In this way, your brain and body communicate, which creates a new neural pathway. Once established, the neural pathway fires automatically in the subconscious part of the brain, and a new habit forms with repetition. As new and positive experiences create new connections in the brain, old connections to undesirable behaviors weaken from a lack of firing.

Awakening Toolkit for Your Journey

Since my toolkit was spare and I had no roadmap for my journey, I am packing both for you. In this book, I've shared an abundance of mindfulness shifts and breathing practices. This chapter has even more tools I've gathered on my awakening journey to accompany you on yours. When I use the word tools in this chapter, the definition, *skills, and knowledge that are useful for a particular purpose or activity,* is the definition I intend. So, you have a toolkit of imaginary tools that remind you to wake up and bring your full attention to the task at hand.

The tools will also help you tune into your body and listen for the messages it has to tell you. Utilizing the concepts of these tools can help you infuse mindful awareness into everyday life situations and support you in sustaining focus and direction. I suggest you start by choosing a breathing practice to work with and one other tool. When you have integrated using that tool, add another tool.

Tools We Are Born With

We begin and end our earthly journey with two gifts – our breath and heartbeat. These are two essential tools to tune into for awakening. You can use your heartbeat and breath in two ways. First, when you experience negative thoughts or a fight, flight, or freeze reaction, it changes your heartbeat and breathing. When you recognize incessant thoughts, you can shift your attention to your breath and do one of the exercises below. Secondly, simple breathing exercises will calm you down when you notice your heartbeat is erratic or racing or you are stressed and anxious. Try both below and use the one that helps the most.

I had a bracelet made with the words, "First, i breathe." When a stressful situation causes me to feel reactionary, this mantra reminds me to pause and take a breath, which releases the tension in my body.

Breath

When mindful of our breath, we are in the present moment. Our breath simply happens, so our practice is to feel the breath entering our body, its movement raising our belly, and then the breath leaving our body. Resting our attention on our breath brings us to a spacious, peaceful place. Use tuning into your breath when you feel stressed, angry, or out of sorts. Also, use it when you want to bring all of you to a task, for instance, when you are getting ready to paint a picture or read a book to your child or grandchild.

Heartbeat

When you have a negative attitude, feel overwhelmed or defensive, shift your focus to the qualities of the heart. The heart exudes unconditional love, compassion, kindness, gratitude, connection, cooperation, and acceptance. Choose a word that helps you with your current challenge. For example, a co-worker was condescending toward you, and now you are fuming. You might pick the phrase, "Accept what is." Once you choose a phrase, use this practice:

- Sit quietly for a minute with your fingers on the pulse in your wrist.
- Breathe slowly and deeply.
- Feel your pulse slow down.
- Wait another minute, then slowly repeat the phrase, "Accept what is."

Breathing Exercises

Do these exercises with your eyes open or closed. Concentrate on relaxing your facial muscles, shoulders, and the rest of your body.

Stress Relief Breath

- Take two breaths through your nose then one long exhale through your mouth.
- Repeat it until you feel relaxed.

Calming Heartbeat Breath

- Use the 4-6 count technique for anxiety, relaxation, and help falling asleep.
- Breathe slowly through your nose for a mental count of four.
- Exhale through your mouth for a count of six.
- Repeat it until you feel relaxed.

Beneficial Mindfulness Tools

Barometer

A barometer is an instrument that measures atmospheric pressure. Similarly, you can use your awareness to 'measure' pressure in your body. When you are stressed, tired, angry, or feel constricted, you experience pressure in the body. This tension can make you feel overly reactive and grumpy. Your breath is likely shallow, your pulse might be elevated, and you are in your mind, not aware of your surroundings. Depending upon the circumstance, you might exhibit signs of a fight-or-flight response or anxiety.

When you feel there are not enough hours in a day, are overwhelmed, have insomnia, or your mood is dark, the barometer exercise will be a beneficial mindfulness tool. Simply bringing awareness to pressure in the body can shift you from ego consciousness into the spaciousness of universal consciousness, where you experience ease and feel expansive. You breathe deep, aware of your surroundings as your heart opens and your mind consciously comes into the present moment.

Now, let's get out the barometer so you can observe how you react to a circumstance at hand. Are you freaking the f**k out, or are you looking for a way to bring some space, peace, and ease into the situation? Do you choose to fight with 'what is,' or do you choose to accept 'what is?'

Let's use this example for practice. You overhear your mother-in-law telling her friend she wishes her son had never married you. You immediately feel your face flushed with anger. You want to yell at her and embarrass her in front of her friend. You grab the phone to call your husband at work. STOP. You remember to use the barometer exercise in your tool kit to get in touch with the pressure in your body. You experience shallow breathing, bubbling anger, a racing heart, and a tight throat. The room feels like it's closing in on you, and your stomach is constricted. You immediately begin to breathe deeply and feel your abdomen rise and fall as you draw your breath to the bottom of your belly. You visualize yourself floating on a raft with the sun warming your body.

You can also give yourself permission to be excused from the family gathering, boil water for chamomile tea, go for a walk, or draw a hot bath. You don't have to worry about what anyone thinks. This saying holds a lot of power and ease, "What other people think of me is none of my business." For those raised with the mantra, "Always be nice," disengaging from a person or toxic situation can feel harsh or abrasive. It's not. It's called a healthy boundary and self-love.

The scenario above can play out several different other ways as well. One way is to get stinking mad when you overhear your mother-in-law, which is understandable. But you can still excuse yourself for twenty minutes to take some space so you can calm down, then decide at another time how you want to handle the situation.

This following scenario, though, ends up becoming toxic not only for you but for those involved. You explode with anger on the spot and tell your mother-in-law to f**k off. Everyone feels the pressure of the situation. Your children hear your outburst and internalize the experience. The mother-in-law retaliates with anger or storms out the door. You call your husband. Now he feels the pressure, but he's busy and can't leave to help you deal with your emotions. So, you call a friend to process the experience and rehash the story, getting more furious by the minute. Everyone involved in the situation is reliving the event and creating stories in their minds to support their "rightness." In the end, the second scenario causes you and others involved to harbor resentment and anger. Incidents like this happen every day between friends, lovers, co-workers, and siblings. Children involved can't fully process what's happened as they experience the pressure and stress in their bodies. Remember to help them process disruptive events by taking responsibility for your part.

The point of using the concept of a barometer is to connect with the pressure in your body and let it remind you to gain distance from your racing mind and run-away emotions. Being reactionary or trying to resolve issues in a heated moment can create suffering for all involved. You can release pressure in the body by breathing, engaging mindfulness, calming the mind, inviting ease, and giving the situation space. When raging emotions have passed, you can mindfully reflect on how you want to address the event and release any remaining emotional charge.

The Kaleidoscope

A kaleidoscope is a tubular-shaped toy designed with pieces of glass and mirror plates. Looking through it, you view a scene as a snapshot. But when you turn it, an endless array of patterns are reflected. Turn it one degree – just one tiny, bitty change – and an entirely different picture comes into view.

With this image in mind, let me ask you, "Do you have expectations about how things "should" turn out? Are you disappointed when someone doesn't respond the way you anticipated? Is change hard for you?"

If so, the kaleidoscope is the perfect mindfulness tool because life is just like a kaleidoscope. The entire universe is turning and changing every second. This is true for your life as well. You may see things one way, but with just a little turn, a slight shift in consciousness, you will see an entirely different "reality." You are giving your life meaning, so why not look for an expansive, loving, positive meaning instead of an angry, contracted, negative one?

Let's use the example of the encounter with a mother-in-law again to practice. Let's say you chose to walk away and take a bath or go for a stroll. Think about the kaleidoscope...how can you turn your view of this situation one little bit to create a new picture, a different reality? There is no way to unhear what your mother-in-law said, so the situation can't be changed.

You can decide that her opinion of you isn't likely to change and stay in the relationship. You can choose to have a very limited relationship with her. If the relationship is extremely toxic, you can talk to a therapist or end your relationship.

Using the concept of turning a kaleidoscope throughout your day can be beneficial. Here's how it works in my life. I woke up today excited to write. With only a few weeks to meet a deadline, I anticipate an uninterrupted day of writing bliss. Ten minutes into writing, I type one line and get the dreaded "not responding" message. I call tech support, and a delightful woman begins working on the issue. The minutes click by – fifteen, thirty, forty-five. I watch dark thoughts drift into my mind, "The last time this happened, I didn't have a computer for three days."

The minute dark thoughts enter, I turn the kaleidoscope. The woman helping me is delightful and determined. What a blessing. The view from my office reveals a large expanse of water, so I joked with her, saying that I was ready to see a dolphin. Just then, two dolphins came into my view. Two hours pass, then two-and-a-half hours pass. I stay in the present, happily talking to Jessica, hopeful she will get to the bottom of the issue, and feel blessed to have a service contract and a beautiful view from my office. I let go of my expectation of a productive writing day. Instead of having three hours of stress and aggravation because life didn't go as expected, I accepted 'what is.' The kaleidoscope offers a choice – stay in a funk or try the view from a different perspective.

Compass

A compass is a navigational and orientation instrument containing a magnetized pointer that shows the direction of the north pole. True north is often referred to as a fixed point in a spinning universe. Metaphorically, true north is the direction of a person's sense of purpose. You get to decide what your true north is. What does your soul most desire? The direction can be as simple as moving in the direction of love, not fear. You can make awakening your true north, and when you're moving in the direction of the ego, remember that awakening is the direction you're moving toward. Take time to focus on your true north. If you are uncertain what your true north is, ask yourself what motivates you to get out of bed in the morning, what lights up your heart and puts a smile on your face, and what are you truly passionate about.

You can use the compass in your toolbelt to stay pointed in the direction of *your* true north as you navigate daily life. These questions help discern which direction you are moving in. When you are not moving in the direction of your true north, shift your energy and mindset to navigate toward your soul's desire.

- Are you walking toward what weighs you down or moving toward what lights you up?
- Do you feel centered, peaceful, and grounded, or is your current state overwhelmed, frenetic, and untethered?
- Are you moving toward love or fear?
- Is your breath rhythmic and moving down into your belly, or is it shallow and rapid?

- Does the food you ingest give you energy and buoyancy or make you feel lethargic?
- Do you feel mutual support from your friends or feel used and depleted?
- Are your home and belongings appreciated and cared for, or are they neglected and overlooked?
- Is your family feeling seen, well-loved, and nurtured, or are they disconnected, rushed, and unnoticed?

Chisel

As Michelangelo said while preparing to sculpt a hunk of marble, "I saw the angel in the marble and carved until I set him free."

We are the angel, the infinite divine energy. Our work is to chip away the hunks of stone...the illusion hiding a higher self. We don't have to find it; we are it. A soulful person spends their life in self-reflection, recognizing thoughts, actions, and beliefs that no longer serve them. With chisel in hand, they patiently observe what needs to be chipped away, removing all that is superfluous and revealing their true essence.

So, what do you need to chip away to reveal your happiness and divinity? What makes you feel rigid? Are you hiding parts of yourself? What boulders are blocking your path to greater awareness? Often, the first thought that pops into your mind contains the answer. Common themes for stumbling blocks are unresolved issues with a relative or failing to be grateful for life's blessings. Don't overlook the nagging little things, the unpaid bill, the stray papers begging to be filed, the unpainted trim on the ceiling. The tiniest thorn in your foot can consume all your mental energy. Imagine the issues that get in the way of your peace and happiness being chipped away.

Speedometer

A speedometer is a device that measures speed. When imagining a speedometer as you go about your day, measure your everyday activities in terms of excessive speed, just right speed, or too slow. Excessive speed blurs magical moments. Have you driven down the interstate at 90 miles per hour? Did you see the wildflowers growing in the median, the graceful heron fishing in the pond, or the ancient, weathered sign announcing gas at 49 cents a gallon?

The speedometer helps you become aware of how you move through your day. When you rush around the house frantically doing chores, you may miss the painful look on your child's face or overlook the plant withering on the dusty shelf. Or are you hampered by inertia, taking up permanent residence on the couch? Remember ways to savor the moment.

Find your inner rhythm by utilizing the questioning process: "Am I lost in thought, or am I aware of my body and surroundings?"

- "Why am I moving so fast?"
- "Why am I moving so slow?"
- "What am I avoiding?"
- "What speed matches my inner rhythm."

Your body is a fine-tuned machine, so make sure it's going at the perfect speed to align with your inner rhythm.

Eraser and Delete Button

When I conduct retreats, I use the concept of editing for every facet of my teachings. If my students are working on art, I have them ask themselves what their gut tells them about what belongs in their art and what needs editing. When they talk, what could be left unsaid? When they eat, what food does their body thrive on, and what food would be better left on the plate? We can use the eraser and delete button as a mindfulness tool to curate what stays and what goes.

Rumi said, "Before you speak, let your words pass through three gates: Is it true? Is it necessary? Is it kind?"

When hurtful words spill from the mouth, they can't be returned. Repercussions from cutting words can have lifetime consequences. Asking Rumi's three questions will help you mentally erase not only harsh but unnecessary words. Just as you can edit the words you write, you'll be well served to edit words before you say them.

Long silent pauses can be uncomfortable and awkward when interacting with people in social situations. Instead of filling dead air with extraneous conversation, ask questions. You will get to know people on a deeper level when you engage in meaningful communication with them.

It's helpful to ask yourself, "Will what I'm going to say enrich the conversation." Another consideration is to ask yourself, "Is what I am about to say relevant to the person I'm about to say it to?" When the person doesn't know Aunt Mary, a long story about Aunt Mary's new home purchase is most likely a good use of the delete button in the brain before the story is told.

Timer

In this modern, digital age, some people live a distracted life in the fast lane. They can buy tons of gadgets to increase efficiency and simplify life while simultaneously adding more tasks to their to-do list. So, it's important to ask, "Am I taking time to ask myself if the items on my list are in alignment with my spirit? Am I frittering away time on the mundane or doing what is inspiring and nurturing?"

A rushed life full of multi-tasking depletes the soil in which you grow. Did you know the brain is wired to do one task at a time? Multi-tasking, then, is *task switching*, going rapidly from one task to another. When you do this, two parts of the brain work against one another. Attempting to do two or three things at once taxes the brain, with each task taking longer than performing the tasks independently. Multi-tasking can make you prone to mistakes and accidents. Going from one task to another burns more glucose, making you feel exhausted. And task-shifting is addictive. Dopamine is released when you complete small tasks like deleting emails, reading texts, or answering phone calls. Instead of sinking your teeth into more meaningful projects, you may have the tendency to do small, inconsequential tasks for the dopamine rush.

When you find yourself multi-tasking, it's the perfect opportunity to address the habit by watching your behavior and course-correct by practicing mindfulness. Here's what it can look like. I am in the habit of making the bed while thinking about doing laundry, menu planning for dinner, and watering the plants. This can go on all day. Before I finish making the bed, I remember I'm waiting for a text and find myself hunting for the phone. So, how does one break the habit of multi-tasking and savor doing one conscious thing at a time? Use a timer.

When setting the timer, be mindful to focus on a single task. Single-tasking helps break the addiction to the dopamine rush received from multi-tasking. It also helps overcome inertia and overwhelm. The whirlwind of multi-tasking can create piles of half-completed tasks, with time spent looking for documents buried beneath a pile of papers or being frazzled because of so many unfinished projects. This can cause anxiety and damage to adrenal glands and to brain cells that store memories. But mindfully completing one task at a time keeps you present, centered, and calm. With practice, single-tasking becomes the norm, and you lose the impulse of habitual behavior, driving you to do several things at once. Slowing down aligns you with a natural rhythm and builds momentum to move toward what feeds you instead of what depletes you.

When you first try single-tasking, expect that maintaining focus can be challenging. Anytime you work on breaking a behavior, your ego puts up a fight. Don't put on boxing gloves. Instead, breathe into the sensation and let it move through your body. It will pass. Avoid judgment if you give in to the feeling and begin multi-tasking, but remember multi-tasking is a worthy habit to break. When you find yourself multi-tasking, engage the Watchful Observer to become aware of what it feels like in your mind and body. Stay committed to practicing single-tasking until it becomes a habit.

Here are ways to improve your ability to complete single tasks.

- Set priorities.
- Be mindful of what you are doing. Bring all your attention to the present moment.
- Clear distractions. When using the internet, open one page at a time on the navigation menu. Put the phone in another room and turn off the TV.
- Plan a specific time to check emails and text messages.
- Set a timer for tasks. Start with 15-minute intervals to build the single-tasking muscle.
- Take a break between tasks.

Creep Meter

A creep meter is an instrument that monitors the movement of active fault lines in the earth. Our trauma creates emotional fault lines, wounds that generate fractures in our inner landscape.

The idea of what a creep meter does can help you connect with your felt sense. We refer to the felt sense or the internal sensations and an inner knowing as gut instinct. It's important to give voice to those sensations that can lead to unresolved emotional issues. Sometimes, there are subtle stirrings in the body that can be described as quickening, pulling, rumblings, constrictions, or jumpiness. Giving these sensations attention enables them to provide information from the subconscious part of the brain that is not recognized by the conscious mind.

While we may not remember traumatic events with the conscious mind, the memory of the event is stored in the body. Instead of being overtaken by impulsive reactions, you can continually practice getting in touch with body sensations and let them move through you. The idea of the creep meter can help you recognize and dialogue with them. When you feel a sensation in your body or can't get a situation out of your head, do the Felt Sense Exercise below.

Felt Sense Exercise

- Find a quiet place to lie down.
- Breathe deep into your belly and release your breath.
- Do this a few times as you let your surroundings fade.
- Let your thoughts flow by. Don't attach to them.

Feel the place in your body that is calling your attention. Stay with that feeling. Give that feeling a descriptive name, like 'jumpy' or 'tightness.' If an image comes up, describe it. For instance, a hand is constricting my heart. Ask a question. For example, if you are addressing tightness, you might ask the tightness, "What do you need to relax?" If you are talking to the hand constricting the heart, you can ask, "Why are you holding my heart so tightly?"

When you are experiencing an emotional reaction, think about the creep meter.

- Where in your body do you feel the disruption, the fractures, the fault lines shifting?
- Did a situation happen that pushed an old reactive button?

You can call on the Watchful Observer and gain a mountaintop view, breathe into the emotion, feel it, and then let it fade.

Fathometer

A fathometer, or sonic depth finder, uses sound to measure the ocean's depth. Invoke the fathometer to gauge the depth of your behaviors, conversations, and relationships with yourself and others. Are your behaviors haphazard or mindful? Are your relationships shallow or deep? Does it feel safe and familiar to play in the shallow end with the ego in control? Do you think you have to give something up to explore a deeper, richer, soulful life? What is calling you from the depths? What are your deep longings?

The concept of the fathometer tool would have helped during my early twenties when my shallow living grated on me like nails on a chalkboard. For the longest time, I was clueless about how to change my trajectory. As I played in the pool's shallow end, the deep end's mysteries beckoned. Insubstantial conversations bored me, meaningless sexual experiences left me empty, and material pursuits held no intrigue. Although drowning in shallow water, I feared the unknown lurking in the depth's darkness.

I quit masking the pain of my emptiness and began to sit with the enormity of its weight. Feeling the weight of my empty life and recognizing my inability to take a risk moved me to action. I dipped my toe in the deep end, which I wrote about at the beginning of this chapter, and found every step exhilarating, holy, and enormously nourishing. I had wallowed in a story that filled me with paralyzing fear when, all along, I had everything I needed to negotiate the murky depths.

Are you ready for one final chapter on how to navigate life like a Zen master, filled with more ease, freedom, and happiness?

You've been presented with lots of information on why all of us do what we do and gained knowledge on how to undo what doesn't sustain a rich, inner life. The last chapter will teach you to weave the wisdom you've gained into the tapestry of your life by practicing awakening through self-reflection. All that is "not you" will fade away.

Since most of what isn't you is damn heavy to lug around, I think you'll enjoy the lightness of the luminous being you're cultivating.

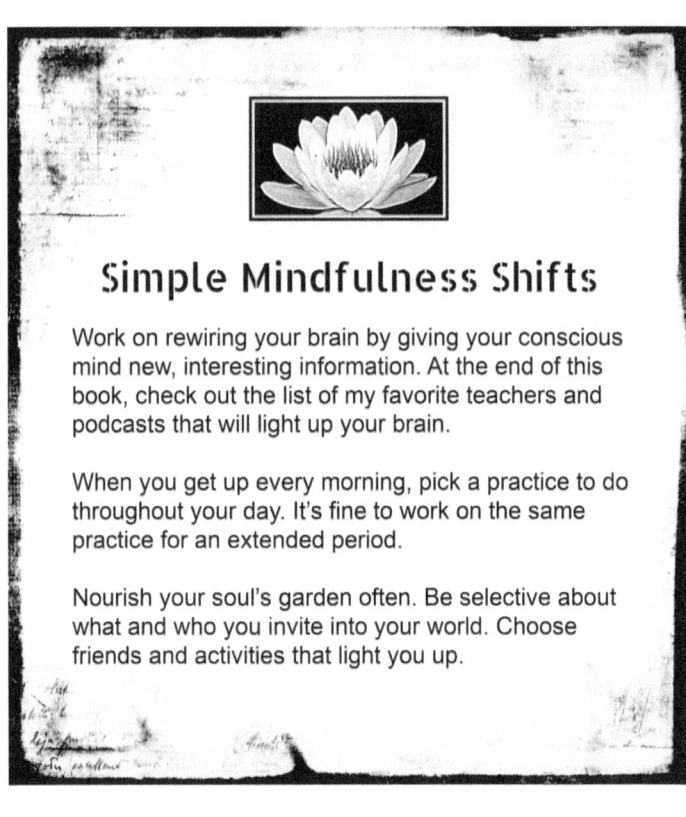

Simple Mindfulness Shifts

Work on rewiring your brain by giving your conscious mind new, interesting information. At the end of this book, check out the list of my favorite teachers and podcasts that will light up your brain.

When you get up every morning, pick a practice to do throughout your day. It's fine to work on the same practice for an extended period.

Nourish your soul's garden often. Be selective about what and who you invite into your world. Choose friends and activities that light you up.

Navigating Everyday Life
Like a Zen Master

"Teachers open the door, but you must enter by yourself."
– Chinese Proverb

Life as Our Guru

My mission is to share wisdom, tools, and a roadmap to illuminate your soul's path, leading to happiness, ease, and awakening. I walk this path not only to create ease in my life but to teach you how to alleviate sufferings pitfalls unnecessarily caused by limiting beliefs and false, unexplored stories we tell ourselves.

These pages are filled with the tools I wish I had known in my twenties when I felt so alone, depressed, and directionless. I didn't realize that my dark night of the soul phase, a search many of us go through, was a quest to find my true north. Releasing everything comfortable and familiar allowed me to surrender to the strong magnetic pull within.

This clarity of mission didn't come overnight. In the past, my greatest desire was to jump from the merry-go-round of self-deprecating thoughts that left me restless and without purpose. Outwardly, I appeared to be happy and high functioning. But inside, I ached for a miracle or magic pill to erase my pain and free my creative spirit so I could experience the reverence and spaciousness I knew as a child. And then, I had the near-death experience I told you about at the book's opening. When I drove off the cliff, my last moments of consciousness let me revisit the vast, spacious oneness I experienced in childhood – our soul's home.

Experiencing spaciousness and ease even when hard stuff happens is a blessing, but how do we find it? Our overactive minds keep us from tapping into spacious awareness, and experiencing it takes practice. During this human journey, shit happens that rocks our world. Our seemingly unwavering trajectory can be turned upside down with one phone call, one medical diagnosis, or one car crossing the solid yellow line.

The mind loves certainty, but life is random and uncertain. Having all the tools in *Roadmap to Ease* at your fingertips isn't enough to find the solid ground of spaciousness within. Having knowledge isn't the same as having an experience. A roadmap is a visual representation of the trajectory you wish to follow. To know the terrain, you must walk the path. Daily practices and self-reflection bring the *Roadmap to Ease* to life. These tools, practices, and thought-provoking questions need to be practiced and pondered. A breathing exercise is no more than words on paper until our attention is on the feeling of air entering our nose and filling our lungs. Only then, when the practices are woven into the fabric of our being, have we developed the equanimity to stand firm when life's tornadoes barrel into us.

The most effective way to deal with life's unpredictability is to practice resting in present awareness.

During the years I've worked on this book, uncertainty has rained down as life brought a barrage of scary and heart-wrenching encounters.

The Universe seems to ask, "Oh, you think you've got this?"

Well, the Universe is conducting a test called "How Do You Handle These Life Situations?"

Each day, I practiced staying in the moment and returning to my breath, keeping worry at bay when possible negative outcomes tried to enter my mind. I observed my reactions to daily circumstances, knowing it is one of my greatest teachers and remembering that life is my guru. I have tested these practices during the most terrifying of times.

A few years ago, my daughter-in-law was rushed to the hospital a month early to deliver my grandchild. She had been diagnosed with a pregnancy-related liver issue, and the doctors determined she had to be induced or lose the baby.

These are the breath-taking moments when wild thoughts can explode, fear gets fanned, and small, scary thoughts become a raging fire that clouds the present moment. Staying in the NOW provides no place for projection or fear to reside. With practice, we quickly remember that being in the NOW is a choice. We can let thoughts recede and observe that presently, all is well. And if later it's not, we will deal with it then.

The premature birth went well, and thankfully, even though my grandson had to stay in the hospital for a week, everyone went home healthy.

Little did I know that one of my greatest fears was about to knock on my door.

A few months after my grandson's early arrival, a fear that lingered for decades appeared on my doorstep, forcing me to confront it head-on. My mother had told me many times that my great-grandfather lost half of his nose to skin cancer. I always feared suffering the same fate because of my childhood spent on the Gulf of Mexico.

My beach girl tribe spent nearly every waking hour swimming and roaming our tropical playground. Years later, it finally caught up with me. Although I had dealt with skin cancer for forty years, I never had surgery on my face. I was diagnosed with skin cancer on the difficult-to-repair part of my nose. My medical condition ignited a couple of years of rapid-fire succession of challenges.

These jarring medical bumps in the road came fast and furious. A large patch of rare skin cancer popped up on my shin. Surgeons made a five-inch incision in my shin and removed a chunk of skin. This resulted in a significant infection that caused unrelenting itching all over my body.

Months went by as I awaited surgery to remove the cancer from my nose. I practiced mindfulness and accepted that I couldn't change the situation. Each day, I practiced staying in the moment and not catastrophizing every possible outcome. The day of surgery arrived, and as my biggest fear unfolded, I listened to a recorded meditation during the procedure. I leaned into the moment, even when the moment meant a blade was taking off pieces of my nose. The doctor had to revisit the site three times before removing all the cancer.

I stayed with my breath, listened to the calming meditations, and left the office many hours later with less of a nose, but a nose nonetheless! Since my nose surgery, I've had at least five surgeries on my face, and two of them were on my nose. A plastic surgeon drilled into my orbital ridge to repair the damage under my eye.

Over the last few years, there have been other losses and heartbreaks. I felt betrayed by friends in my beloved community. One of my childhood best friends died. Other long relationships abruptly ended. My brother and I sold our Maine cottage, which had been in the family for over 60 years. My connection to my childhood and the richness of generational friendships and gatherings ended.

My son and I lived in an intentional, now four-generational community that was my heart's home for 32 years. I expected to live there until my final breath, but the cards have, at least for now, dealt a different hand, and I sold my home a couple of years ago. The transitory nature of life brings many profound lessons, none more significant than the constant beat of change. From moment to moment, the drumbeat keeps a constant tempo of endings, endings, endings.

And speaking of endings, I haven't shared my recent and second near-death experience!

Walking to my car to go to a Graham Nash concert in St. Petersburg at the end of 2023, I stepped down a slight incline and felt a sensation in my leg, but I didn't give it much thought. The next morning, my leg was swollen and throbbing. Days later, I went to the emergency room. The doctor suspected an ACL tear but told me to wait and see if the swelling would go down. After a month of being bedridden and unable to drive, an MRI revealed an ACL tear and a pool of blood behind my knee. Surgery was performed to remove the blood and repair the ACL. Three days later, in pain and with a heavy immobilizing metal leg brace from my knee to my ankle, the hospital released me at 9:30 p.m., and I was transported to a rehab facility.

The staff did not appreciate my late arrival, which began a six-hour nightmare. Since I was not mobile, I requested assistance to go to the bathroom, and the aides didn't come back to assist me, although I could hear them talking outside my room. I have hyponatremia, a condition where there is not enough sodium in the blood. It is deadly if not caught in time. I could feel my sodium dropping and kept pushing the call button, a seemingly ineffective device of thin plastic half-inflated with air. Half an hour ticked by, and I continued to push the call button. Another hour passed. I called for help and shouted that I would die if I didn't get to a hospital.

I could hear the aides laughing and saying, "She thinks she is going to die."

No help came. I kept pushing the call button. Two hours went by, and my thirst level was unbearable. I could no longer think straight, a symptom of severe hyponatremia, but I did have the presence at 5 a.m. to call 911 and tell them I wasn't safe.

As the paramedics rushed me out of the facility, the "mean girls" mocked me. They told the paramedics nothing was wrong with me, and they were sorry I was wasting their time.

Luckily, the hospital was minutes away, and they admitted me quickly as my sodium levels revealed severe hyponatremia. This causes brain swelling, resulting in stroke or death. I called friends to advocate for me. They came to my private room and watched as a medical team assessed my situation. I could feel my body shutting down and my life energy slipping away. More staff came to assist. I told the nurses my bladder was about to burst, and they confirmed it to be true. As people worked on me, I felt suspended between worlds. The invitation to enter spaciousness was inviting and familiar – just like my experience after driving off the cliff.

And then I heard the words, "You've got shit to do." I knew the reference meant there would be no dying before finishing my book.

I was whisked off to the ICU. I remained in the hospital for almost a week as doctors ran tests and steadily increased my sodium.

During these medically challenging years of "testing time," more appropriately called life, I found humor and humility in my vulnerable state. My heart was filled with profound gratitude for my friends and my son, who tended to my needs, and the medical staff who put me back together.

I avoided labeling these challenges as good or bad. When scary thoughts would momentarily crowd my mind like a 5 p.m. New York City subway car, I practiced watching them from a distance. Looking back, I only briefly ran with catastrophizing thoughts or created mental dramas. Ultimately, all had come around right; I had my life, leg, nose, and sanity. Also, I was acutely aware of the distant past when family matters, health, or work issues had turned me into a ball of reactivity and worry. But, over time, the tools I had assimilated on my life's journey were readily available. I could rest easy by practicing meditation and consciously stepping into each present moment, even during tenuous times. Resting in spacious awareness enveloped me in peace and thankfulness.

Sometimes, stressful situations rain down on us; other times, we worry about things that *might* happen. The trick is not to get swept away by fear. Stay firmly planted in the present. Undoubtedly, there will be daily bumps that knock you off-center. Distressing events will threaten your well-being and break your heart. Fights with friends, times when your children's safety is at risk, your income is threatened, or you're fearful that a pandemic may end your life will compromise your peace. You can spend time worrying about these kinds of situations, or you can be present when life is hard; breathe into your distress and focus on releasing the fear, anticipation, expectations, or terror.

When you experience a tragic loss, a myriad of feelings well up. Grief comes in waves, and healing from loss is a process that has its own time clock. Rather than being consumed by the story of your loss, feel the pain, depression, hurt, and anger. Don't ignore or judge these feelings. Try not to numb them or run from them; simply sit with them. And when the feelings move through you, you can experience deep healing even while you grieve.

What Can Trip You Up and How to Avoid Stumbling

It's easy to sail through life when the wind is at your back, but when headwinds barrel into you, it can feel like you're climbing Mt. Everest with a 50-pound backpack. Your endurance and resilience *will* be tested. Every ounce of resistance exerted to keep bad things from happening will not change the tenuousness of the human condition. When stressors occur, will you meet challenging moments with surrender, or will you mask the pain with familiar distractions and dramatic stories and continue the struggle? Will you hop on the emotional roller coaster of life and ride it white-knuckled with a racing heart, or will you find your breath, quiet your mind, and view the challenge from the vantage point of an astronaut observing Earth from space?

Expect to get tripped up. Why? Because you've been conditioned to engage in the struggle – we all have been. We're wired for it. We return to what's familiar, even when it's uncomfortable or painful. But the next time you feel like you may be getting tripped up, it *can* be different. You've learned to step back and not get lost in the struggle.

If you want to revisit what trips you up as well as the awakening skills and practices, the chapters are outlined here so the information is easily accessible.

In Trail Marker 1, *Waking Up to Your Divinity*, we discussed the unhealthy ego traits that, if left unchecked, can trigger frustration, defensiveness, and anger. You want to recognize when you're lost in erroneous beliefs and conditioned behavior patterns and choose to cultivate a healthy ego exuding kindness, curiosity, and authenticity. As you connect with your soulful self, you'll recognize the difference between what you think makes you happy and what truly makes you happy.

Understanding brain functions and the energetic activities of the mind are addressed in Trail Marker 2, *Why Wake Up?* Since you know the subconscious mind operates on autopilot 95%

of the time, reviewing how your habitual behavior trips you up is extremely helpful. To grow spiritually, we don't want to act on autopilot; we want to act and respond from our conscious mind. Other brain functions that cause us to stumble are also addressed in this chapter, and the shifts to awaken from auto-pilot are shared throughout *Roadmap to Ease*.

Clear the Path to Enlightenment is the first shift introduced in Trail Marker 3. Using this shift, you combed through your past to find the beliefs and behaviors that kept you tethered to the ego and did a ritual to release them. Stay mindful of those stumbling blocks and revisit this exercise whenever you want to release the current challenge weighing you down.

In Trail Marker 4, the second shift, *Become the Watchful Observer,* you learned the cost of an undisciplined mind and how to distance yourself from its wild wanderings. It taught you to continually watch your thoughts, emotions, beliefs, and behaviors and notice when they have control. Developing this observation skill gives you the ability to determine when you are lost in thought or when you have distance from your thoughts. With practice, the mind's narration recedes, and you experience more of life in the present.

In the third shift presented in Trail Marker 5, I gave you exercises for *Living in the NOW*. These exercises teach you how to dial into present-moment awareness by questioning where your attention is focused. You no longer must experience life through the narration of the chatty mind. Remember to shift your consciousness, which disengages you from distractions, feelings of restlessness, and projections. They are the tripwires that keep you in the past and future. This chapter teaches you to continually practice mindfulness and breathing, explore spaciousness, tune into bodily sensations, and spend time in nature. It drops you into pure consciousness, a greater sense of awareness, and connects with your ever-present divinity.

Continuing your journey in Trail Marker 6, you explored the fourth shift, *Bravely Ask Good Questions*. You experience unnecessary suffering when you are unaware of making assumptions, having expectations, and getting tripped up by unhealthy ego characteristics. You reclaim your childhood curiosity by asking better questions about your inner workings. This helps you understand why you do what you do and unravels the layers of illusion that obscure your divinity. You've learned to deepen relationships by being brave enough to ask people how they think and feel instead of assuming you already know. Pulling good questions from your parenting toolkit will enrich your connection with your children as well.

In the fifth and final shift, *Nourish Your Body, Mind, and Spirit*, Trail Marker 7 offers simple activities that feed your soul and provide nutrients to fortify spiritual alignment in daily life, even in the face of challenges. Continually enrich the soil in which you plant deep roots. Your life is built on shifting sand, and everything is constantly changing. If you stay deeply rooted like sea oats, you're less likely to be uprooted during life's turbulent times.

In Trail Marker 8, *The Awareness Toolkit*, you use your imagination to conjure up tools that prove invaluable on your awakening journey. And please don't forget my favorite, the kaleidoscope, a metaphor for how we can make a simple shift and view a situation completely differently. This chapter is full of practices, wisdom, and questions to ask yourself that will thaw frozen beliefs and chisel away the illusion blocking your luminous essence.

As you observe your reactions to daily events, familiar themes will begin to emerge. You know you're wired for negative thinking, so watch nagging thoughts with eagle eyes. Your workaround is to rewire your brain, and I walked you through this process in Trail Marker 2 and Trail Marker 8. Pain avoidance is another big stumbling block on your path to enlightenment. When you recognize your pain and the uneasiness of suppressed emotions, feel the feelings and let them move through you.

Another trip hazard is attachment to the ego 'self,' the 'who' you believe yourself to be. It can be disorienting to experience your perception of yourself starting to dissolve. But as you continue to practice being the Watchful Observer, ego characteristics that contribute to your life dramas disappear. Only your divine inheritance, conscious awareness, remains.

Think of Trail Marker 9 as the sign at the trailhead identifying, in this case, where you have been so you can easily return to the places you want to revisit. Hopefully, you will keep *Roadmap to Ease* on your coffee table. I find that reading it with a strong cup of cold brew or a relaxing cup of tea is a perfect pairing, depending on the time of day.

Daily Life is the Practice

We are hardwired to resist change, yet change is the only constant. Our ego's human journey is built on quicksand, which is alarming since we search for certainty, and it's nowhere to be found. This we cannot change. But by practicing mindfulness, we can learn to stand in the face of life's unknowns, the uncertainty, the pain, the confusion, and our resistance to 'what is.' We can breathe into it, feel it, let emotions come, and breathe deeper. Don't label them as good or bad. Name the feelings or emotions as you experience them: that's fear, that's longing, that's thoughts, that's excitement, that's ease, that's disbelief. Give them space to be. They, as everything does, will pass.

Because everything exists within universal consciousness, whether we experience it or not, it can be said that we already walk a spiritual path. The question becomes, do you recognize when you are awake to your divinity? Do you also watch yourself when you're entangled in ego reality? The moment you observe your thoughts and reactions from a distance, you are awakening. This subtle shift in vantage point is a profound transformation. This awakening alone is immeasurable and offers a deep soul connection and a feeling of ease.

The more you move into spaciousness, the more aware you become of the transient nature of all things. So, the separate self you believe to be contained within skin, blood, bones, and inner psychological landscape comes into question. Your lifelong identity will gradually transform as you become less tethered to ego and acutely aware of fabricated life stories that cause unnecessary suffering. You will be clear-eyed when you engage in moments of anger, jealousy, or frustration. You can quickly shift from being lost in volatile emotions to resting in ever-available ease and freedom. When you relax into spaciousness and mindfully watch from the seat of the Watchful

Observer, your heart opens, your mind quiets, your body relaxes, and you are blanketed in tranquility.

Our modern world is filled with shiny objects that constantly distract us. Therefore, it takes commitment to slow down and focus. Simple practices done throughout the day yield worthy insights without requiring an enormous time investment. You will recognize patterned behaviors and triggers and observe all that is fleeting. Mindfulness practices also shine a light on ways you engage suffering, which eclipses a happy, creative life. Things that light you up and bring you peace are also illuminated. Just carry on your day as usual, inviting awareness of the Watchful Observer to join you.

If you do a short meditation before getting out of bed, you will find it's a beautifully gentle way to wake up. Instead of beginning your day outward focused, you connect to your inner rhythm. You can also start your day by setting the intention to remain present and grounded. Short phrases like "I accept what is" or "I practice presence" are helpful mantras to recite throughout the day.

Being rooted in your body connects you to the flow of universal creativity and divine energy. Mindfully returning to your breath is a perfect practice to shift your attention from thoughts to the present. Feel your breath come in through your nose and travel down the back of your throat, filling your lungs and belly, then relax into the exhale. You can say "let be" on the inhale and "let go" on the exhale. Experience the pause between your breaths and the space around thoughts or feelings.

The Whitman's Sampler of Daily Practices

The *Roadmap to Ease* is your companion on your inner journey, abundant with practices, shifts, and questions to ponder. To ease your way down the path to enlightenment, consider these simple practices food for your mind and soul. Just as eating a healthy diet and exercise feeds your body, a daily mindfulness diet rewires your brain and enriches the soul.

Don't get caught in the undertow of overwhelm on the awakening path. Pick one practice from the buffet of choices and savor it like the perfect chocolate you chose from Whitman's Sampler box. Stay with that practice until you embody the teaching. Don't try to do everything all at once. Practice awakening with ease and receptivity without an end game in mind.

Choosing a Practice

There are no wrong choices when picking a practice, shift, or contemplative question. They will all reveal information that is fodder for reflection. Committing to meditating, even for five minutes daily, will fan your devotion and build discipline muscles. Your dedication will result in self-compassion, growing awareness, and emotional regulation.

By practicing the following, you will clear out the cloudy content of your mind. In spaciousness, you clearly see the patterns, stories, beliefs, and opinions that have kept you tangled. Your mind and body start to unwind, and you grow in compassion toward yourself and others. When emotionally distressing events occur, regrets from the past return, or you feel depressed and anxious, know you can sit with the feelings until they pass. You are no longer reactive for long periods and won't get lost in a story you'll endlessly rehash.

Pick a Practice…Any Practice

This is a go-to list when choosing a practice, shift, or question to focus on for a day, week, year, or lifetime. Whether you are new to observing your reactions to daily life situations or a seasoned seeker, keep practices simple. Start with just one practice so you can develop a habit that will yield results. Baby steps toward awakening will yield quantum leaps.

- Bring your attention to your breath.
- Open *Roadmap to Ease* to any page and pick the first practice you see.
- Choose a mantra that addresses an issue you're working on and recite it throughout the day.
- Memorize what the AWAKEN acronym teaches and pick one of the six practices to focus on until you feel like moving to another teaching.
- Pick a question from the three listed below and ask yourself which direction you are moving in and how it makes you feel. Glean the lessons you learn from your observations.

Ask Yourself Throughout the Day

Roadmap to Ease is full of questions to assist you on your awakening journey. Pick any question in the book to use as a daily focus. If you feel struggle or resistance, choose one of these three questions to ground yourself and assess when you are returning to your inner self.

- Am I moving in the direction of ego or divinity?
- Am I coming from a place of fear or love?
- Does what I'm focused on weigh me down or light me up?

Daily AWAKEN Practice

Who doesn't love a great acronym? And what better acronym for a book about waking up than AWAKEN!

Memorize its meaning and use this practice often to facilitate your awakening. Remember two intentions when navigating everyday life like a Zen master: a nonjudgmental, curious demeanor and an attitude of ease. You can spend today however you choose, so why not choose to be mindful of where your attention is focused? Once you dial into your attention, observe: Is what I am focused on nourishing my soul or draining my energy?

The Daily AWAKEN Practice

A — Accept 'What Is' – You can't change what events happened in the past. You can accept the things you cannot change, change the things you can, and have the wisdom to know the difference.

W — Wake Up to the Watchful Observer – Watch your reactions to thoughts, feelings, emotions, and behaviors and how you respond to daily life situations. These observations offer insight into rote behaviors from the past and reveal what triggers you. Trail Marker 4 is your go-to chapter to gain distance from everything transient. All that remains is conscious awareness, a deliciously peaceful place to reside.

A — Ask Good Questions – Being curious about yourself and your interactions with others provides a treasure trove of information, enabling you to investigate what clouds awareness. Curiosity gets us out of habitual behaviors and thoughts by providing new information. This engages our conscious mind, which rewires the brain. Trail Marker 6 is devoted entirely to encouraging you to bravely ask good questions.

K — Keep What Lights You Up – Remember running in the rain as a child, spending endless time building forts and frolicking in nature? Investigate the things that bring you joy, peace, and happiness – and do more of them. Trail Marker 3 helped you excavate what makes you want to happy dance, bringing you a sense of buoyancy and freedom.

E — Edit What Weighs You Down – Trail Marker 3 also helped you identify the things that weigh you down. When your observations illuminate what you want to release, remember to perform the healing ritual to unshackle yourself from detrimental beliefs.

N — Nourish Your Soul's Garden – Nurture your body, mind, and spirit with meditation, walks in nature, and nutritious food. Surround yourself with loved ones. Find your tribe, gain wisdom, love yourself, forgive, and forgive some more. Listen to podcasts, journal, crank up the music, build an altar, and create something. Dance outside your comfort zone, be your biggest cheerleader, breathe in freedom, and co-create your true north with the divine. Find all the things that provide daily sustenance in Trail Marker 5.

Welcome to Freedom, Peace, and Happiness

Picking up *Roadmap to Ease* and reading it to the end demonstrates that you are committed to waking up. You may have been walking awakening's path for years, even decades, before you began to read this book. Maybe you are new to this journey. Chances are you've heard a distant whisper or had an inner knowing that there is more to life than you realized. And now you know it is entirely possible to alleviate unnecessary suffering, lead a happier life, and consciously navigate the path to enlightenment while simply engaging in day-to-day activities. You will gain tremendous insight from watching your reactions or responses to daily life situations. This is your greatest teacher.

You have learned to view the ego's illusions from the spacious presence of the Watchful Observer. You know you are not your thoughts and that they spontaneously come into your mind. You've learned how to disengage from thoughts, so they recede. They are not the boss of you! You also know how to let your feelings move through you. Your sense of duality will continue to fade as you practice mindfulness and notice where your attention resides. If your attention is somewhere unpleasant, anxious, or stressful, you have the choice to shift your focus.

Paying attention to life's dance is one of your most excellent teachers. Is your rhythm frenetic or flowing? Are you inhabiting the present moment or lost in thought? Remember, life is your guru. As you navigate each day and respond to unfolding events, you write the chapters in the book called "My Life."

You don't have to add anything to your life to become enlightened. Waking up is the transitory nature of everything. The content of our daily life is experienced as our thoughts, feelings, activities, and body. The content's transitory nature unfolds in the context of ever-present, infinite awareness. When you tune into ever-present awareness, you observe the content of your experience without judgment. In each moment, you can choose to pay attention to thoughts and behaviors that don't serve you, breathe into the resistance, and observe the demanding ego recede into spacious awareness. *This is the path to enlightenment.*

Any one of us can become our own shaman, medicine man, and medicine woman. As you do the daily practices taught in *Roadmap to Ease*, the demands of your unruly mind will relax its grip. Unexamined stories from your upbringing, believed to be accurate, will melt like ice cubes on hot pavement. As you continue these lifetime practices, divinity will sparkle like diamonds in your eyes, lovingkindness will beat in your heart, and your expanding awareness will reveal the universal oneness that is the essence of your being.

Welcome home.

Muddy and Perfect

I do not wash my hands
between blending pastel colors
Life's too short
and the colors get muddied a bit
Life's like that

Pure colors are not for me
Perfection, a faulted theory
Unless, of course, every moment is seen as perfect
even when it's muddied, messy, bloody, dead
Life is like that
Muddy and perfect

e'Layne Kelley

Let's Stay Connected

Thank you so much for joining me on this journey. I hope *Roadmap to Ease* brought you insight and inspiration.

Your support means the world to me. You've been on my mind and heart over the years I've worked on this book. Although I don't know you personally, our divine oneness binds us. Our stories have different themes, but the challenges of daily life spare few. One thing is for sure: we share the desire for love and connection.

So, let's stay connected.

Please feel free to ask me questions and share stories about any insight or aha moments you experienced from reading *Roadmap to Ease*.

Here are a couple of gifts for you.

Download my free 24-page arty eBook – 7 Mindfulness Shifts to Gain Distance from Negative Thoughts. The download button is on the front page of www.eLayneKelley.com.

As a thank you for buying my book, here is an 8x10 ready-to-frame art print you can download with a great message – What do you want to pack for your life's journey…what do you want to leave behind? www.eLayneKelley.com/artprint/

You can reach me here:

I am on many social media platforms. Instead of bombarding you with links, go to my website, where you'll find all the hotlinks.

- ◎ Email: eLayneKelley@gmail.com
- ◎ Website: www.eLayneKelley.com
- ◎ Private Facebook Group: www.facebook.com/groups/ gainthewisdomsisterhoodtribe

You can also sign up for my newsletter, which shares info about upcoming classes and book signings.
I am also available to speak at conferences and provide virtual coaching.

May we all continue to release what weighs us down and embrace what lights us up.

Wisdom Teachers

Adyashanti, Rupert Spira, and Eckhart Tolle's wisdom feeds my heart and soul. They convey the nature of pure consciousness in simple language and share profound spiritual teachings on YouTube. Their books are available on Amazon, Audible, and local bookstores.

Inspiring Podcasts

These hosts interview many accomplished coaches, authors, scientists, entrepreneurs, and those pushing the boundaries of what is possible. They pose thoughtful questions, mining a treasure trove of information to empower, inspire, stretch, motivate, and excite their listeners. Some subjects discussed are health, mindset, entrepreneurship, spirituality, and healing from trauma.

Lewis Howes – School of Greatness

Rich Roll – The Rich Roll Podcast

Tom Bilyeu – Impact Theory

Brilliant Teachers

I've enjoyed attending workshops and taking classes from many of these teachers. They generously impart their wisdom and are passionate, big-hearted, creative humans with a mission to share: Bruce Lipton, Tony Robbins, Dean Graziosi, Oprah, Gabby Bernstein, Jack Canfield, Brene Brown, Elizabeth Gilbert, Tracy Verdugo, Patricia Wooster, Wendi Blum Weiss, Melissa Ricker, Joe Dispenza, Jack Kornfield, Brendon Burchard, and Mel Robbins. I love waking up to A Note from the Universe, written by Mike Dooley.

www.ingramcontent.com/pod-product-compliance
Lightning Source LLC
Chambersburg PA
CBHW020228130626
46549CB00005B/1786